ANY NIGHT GRILLING

FOOD52

ANY NIGHT GRILLING

60 WAYS TO FIRE UP DINNER (AND MORE)

Paula Disbrowe

Photography by
James Ransom

TEN SPEED PRESS
California | New York

Contents

DOUGH

CHEESE

CHARRED GREENS & SMOKY SALADS

GRILLED & COAL-ROASTED VEGETABLE MAINS

FRESH CATCHES

BARBECUED BIRDS & JUICY PORK

BEEF, BURGERS & LAMB

Foreword

Years ago, my husband and I visited my friend Paula and her husband, David, on the ranch they were running in Texas Hill Country. Between collecting eggs from their hens, feeding the horses, and running their dogs, she and David casually slow-roasted goat over an open fire for dinner. I don't do this kind of thing, but I like attaching myself to friends who do.

I have always believed in surrounding myself with people I look up to. With one friend, I admire her relentless determination. With another, his Google-like brain. With Paula, I have long been in awe of her ease in the kitchen (her sly joke cracking, too). It's as if she were born not with a silver spoon in her mouth but tongs in her hands.

When Merrill Stubbs, Food52's cofounder, and I were dreaming up this book, Paula naturally leapt to mind. We wanted a grilling cookbook that wouldn't be like every other chest-pounding, aggressively typefaced, you're-a-wuss-if-you-don't-cook-a-whole-pig cookbook on the market. These books don't speak to us. They make us feel bad about our Webers. They make us resent grilling.

And, yet, we love grilled food! We'd like to do more grilling! We'd even do it on weeknights if you'd show us how to make it approachable!

We knew if anyone could pull this off, Paula could. She'd pour us a drink, put on some Waylon Jennings, and casually coach us to toss some halloumi on the hot grates. It would all seem like a dream—and no big deal.

And that's just what happened. Paula got us making nachos, but with grilled corn. She showed us how to smoke tomatoes for an earthy lentil soup (see page 107). We'll soon be serving our crisped chicken wings with a pretense-free Cholula butter (see page 138). And we're already planning a dinner around the El Rancho grilled pizza (see page 36), a spunky pie topped with shaved zucchini, ricotta, and mint.

There is a place in the world for cooks like us to love our grill. And we can all thank Paula—our Susan B. Anthony of the grill—for helping us find our way here.

—Amanda Hesser, cofounder of Food52

Introduction: Why Grill? (It's More Fun with Fire)

Like all good stories, this one begins over a bed of smoldering coals, with a cold libation and a playlist shuffle of Texas troubadours. That scenario—with the addition of family, friends, and a couple of lazy ranch dogs snoozing nearby—is my happy place. There are few things I love more than cooking outside on a cool evening, watching the light fade while listening to the snap and pop of a fire coming to life. But I'm getting ahead of myself.

First, a confession. I began this book as a "weekend griller." I'm no stranger to building fires—when my husband, David, and I spent four years cooking on a ranch in the Texas Hill Country, they were a daily affair. But when it came to grilling dinner, I could get the job done (knocking out a couple of rib eyes, for instance), though it took a fair amount of planning, and I would be riddled with self-doubt during the process. That's primarily because of our established roles and how our work was divided early on. David typically got the job of manning the grill, while I whisked vinaigrettes, shook skillets, juggled kids and guests, and stirred cocktails (not necessarily in that order). I've always gravitated to the sensual pleasures of a fire, but it was usually later, after my kitchen tasks were complete. For this book, we swapped roles. I signed on to several months of backyard cooking, and David graciously (if somewhat reluctantly) held down the fort inside.

And so began several months of arriving home with my kids around five and then hustling to grill dinner before their bedtime. What started as a scramble soon developed into a smoother rhythm, with smarter game plans and the recipes in this book. Before long, it became routine to light a chimney of charcoal soon after I walked through the back gate, which gave me about thirty minutes until the red-hot coals were ready to be poured onto the cooking grate to prep the meal.

With only a few exceptions, the recipes in this book don't require overnight marinades or lengthy, low-and-slow cook times. Every now and then I'm organized enough to, say, marinate meat in the morning so it's ready to go that evening. This feels less like a chore than a small thrill, because I anticipate the meal in a different way, knowing that when I get home after a long day, deeply flavored chicken drumsticks (or some such) are ready to roll. But for the most part, I rely on anything (from cabbage to shrimp to slices of cheese) that can be grilled quickly and doesn't require many other components to create a meal. That's one of the major benefits of grilling: The crisp textures and complexity of the charred and caramelized flavors mean that you don't need much embellishment. After one bite of crispy, grill-roasted chicken, you'll know exactly what I mean.

Grilling provides other benefits beyond flavor. Cooking outside several nights a week shifted the dynamic of our family dinners. It's hard not to feel happy when you're enjoying the colors of a softening sky, the rustle of a breeze stirring pecan branches, and the aroma of fat pork chops sizzling on the grill. My kids spent more time in the backyard. Music practice moved outdoors. We entertained more often because the laid-back nature of "dinner on the grill" diffused the stress and usual expectations (for me at least) of having people over.

The most exciting result of frequent and enthusiastic grilling is that it opens a delicious world of possibility, particularly once you begin to think beyond burgers and steaks (although they still rank among our favorites). Grilling deepens the intrigue of vegetables, creates a crackly crust for pizza, and infuses everything from scallions to swordfish with an irresistible charred flavor. And grilling is resourceful: It revives less-than-fresh bread, intensifies the natural sweetness of fruits and vegetables, and often provides a lingering heat that allows you to "cook ahead" by prepping components for future meals.

On the following pages, you'll discover that the most crave-worthy take-out flavors (from spicy wings to Asian beef) are even better prepared at home. Suddenly, everything—from the obscure vegetable in your CSA basket to the wild mushrooms at the market—will get your wheels turning. The cuts of meat and glimmering whole fish that may have dropped from your radar will now be full of inspiration. You don't need to embark on barbecue boot camp; just read on and dig in to the recipes in this book. Whether you enjoy them on the back porch or in your dining room, I hope they'll inspire countless happy meals around your table.

fact that you'd be hard-pressed to find a similar model outside the land of armadillos and drive-through beverage barns), it wasn't an option for *Any Night Grilling*.

It was clear that grilling on a Tuesday required a gas grill and/or a kettle-style charcoal grill with a cover. Our friend Aaron Franklin, the revered pitmaster and brisket whisperer behind Franklin's Barbecue in Austin, turned me on to PK Grills (aka Portable Kitchen), an Arkansas-based manufacturer that's been around since the 1950s. The PK360 is the right model grill for me because of its unique capsule shape, which maximizes cooking space and makes building a fire with two temperature zones easier and more intuitive; its four-point venting system, which helps to control airflow to maintain consistent heat; and a hinged cooking grate—super-handy when you need to add charcoal for longer cooking times.

To decide which grill is right for you, you'll need to take a personality test of sorts to match up your priorities (speed and control or flavor and sport?) with the appropriate option. A top-of-the-line model is fun, stylish, and more flexible, but it's not necessary. The truth is, with the right technique and fuel and the best ingredients, you can get great results from an inexpensive kettle (remember that much of the world grills delicious food every day on a rustic setup). For the most versatility, buy the largest grill your budget allows, and be sure it's a model with a cover that lets you both grill-roast and smoke, two techniques that deliver awesome flavor.

Except for a few preparations—like the Smoky Ratatouille (page 96) and Rebel Tomahawk (page 193) which require hot, glowing embers—the recipes in this book can be prepared on either a charcoal or gas grill. Both create charred flavors that are hard to replicate indoors. But there are significant differences in the results.

Firing Up the Grill

———

To kick things off, this section will cover a few basics, like choosing and setting up a grill, troubleshooting grill conundrums, and more tips that will improve your grill game so you can knock out a meal with confidence.

CHARCOAL VS. GAS: WHICH GRILL IS FOR YOU?

Before I dove into this book, my husband and I relied on a rustic grill that's common in South Texas, a large, heavy round with a hinged grate that can be raised or lowered, and swung over or away from the fire. It's an object that beckons guests to gather around to swap stories and watch logs burn to ashes, but without a cover, controlling the heat is a challenge. For that reason (and the

Charcoal

What's to love: deep smoky flavors, the excitement of a live fire

Once I started cooking on my PK Grill, my gas model was seriously neglected. I'm a charcoal junkie and love the interactive challenge and sport of cooking over a fire. Because factors like the weather, the wind, and the charcoal or wood make each fire unique, the process is slightly different every time, and that's precisely why it's fun.

Gas

What's to love: speed, control, reliability

When it comes to fast cooking, gas grills are a true game changer. Turn a few dials, push a button, and *whoosh*—smoking hot grates in minutes. The process is so easy that sometimes I fire mine up just to char tortillas or grill late-night chicken breasts for lunch boxes the next day. But most gas grills don't get as hot as charcoal grills, and the internal temperature drops dramatically when you raise the lid. The biggest difference in the outcome, however, is flavor: Gas grills just don't infuse foods with the same deep, chargrilled goodness that cooking over a live fire provides. Sear a steak or burger on both grills and you'll taste the difference.

If you choose a gas grill, there are ways to work with it for optimal results:

Keep it clean: A clean grill cooks more evenly and will deliver the best flavor—you want your food to be charred by hot grates, not blackened by a layer of soot that creates an off-flavor.

Preheat before cooking: To replicate the high-heat impact generated by a hot fire, heat a closed grill for 10 to 15 minutes before cooking.

Keep it closed: To retain the intense ambient heat that cooks food quickly and evenly, open the grill only when necessary.

Enhance flavor: Low-and-slow barbecue isn't an option on weeknights, but you can create a similar effect in a fraction of the time by allowing wood chips (see page 11) or hearty sprigs of fresh herbs (in a smoker box or perforated aluminum foil packet) to smolder over the heat.

Grill Pan

Where does a grill pan fit into the pantheon of options? When the weather isn't cooperating or you're in a pinch, you can use a grill pan on your stove top to create similar results, with everything from breakfast sausage to vegetables. Your best bet is a heavy, enamel-coated cast-iron model, which cooks evenly and maintains an even heat. The ridges on the bottom create sear marks and elevate food above the drippings. Grill pans are particularly well suited for quick-cooking items like chicken breasts, lamb chops, firm cheeses, and vegetables. What you don't get, of course, is the ambient heat and deeper flavors created by a live fire.

PICKING YOUR FUEL

The source of your fire affects the flavor of your food, so know your options (and read those bags carefully) to pick the one that's right for you.

Lump Charcoal

Like most chefs, I prefer irregularly shaped lump hardwood charcoal that's made by burning whole logs or large pieces of wood in a kiln without oxygen. The result is a pure product made from various types of hardwood (oak, mesquite, and hickory) that burns cleaner, hotter, and longer than products made with chemical additives or fillers. As a result, the subtle and natural flavors of food cooked over fire are allowed to shine. My favorite brand (for quality and vintage-inspired packaging) is B&B, which stands for Better Burning.

Briquettes

A buddy of mine prefers briquettes because they're uniformly shaped and easy to light, and their burn is steady and consistent. Briquettes are made from charcoal and other ingredients like compressed sawdust molded together with paraffin or petroleum binders (though natural briquettes are made from pulverized charwood held together with natural starches). The added ingredients create an ashier burn, so they don't get as hot, and briquettes lack the distinct flavor of lump charcoal.

Instant Charcoal

They start quickly because they're soaked in lighter fluid and other chemical additives that affect the flavor of food (I don't use them).

Gas

Gas grills run on liquid propane, available in tanks at supermarkets and hardware stores, and natural gas. Most newer models come with propane gauges, a handy way to know when you're running low on fuel (and avoid last-minute dashes to the store for a replacement tank before a dinner party).

SETTING UP YOUR GRILL

What follows is a step-by-step guide to setting up a grill, from lighting the coals to oiling the hot grates. Flip the page for some handy visuals.

Step 1: Light the Fire

The best way to light a fire for a charcoal grill is with a charcoal chimney (also called a chimney starter). To do this, place some scrunched newspaper (or paper bags) in the bottom compartment and fill the top canister with coals (see next page). Then tilt the chimney slightly to encourage airflow and light the paper with a match. Give the paper a few seconds to catch, then stand the chimney upright and let it do its thing. If the coals don't catch, no worries; just add more paper and try again.

About 15 minutes after you light the paper, flames will appear at the top of the chimney. Your charcoal is now lit well enough to be dumped onto the bottom grate and spread or banked, depending on what you're going to cook. For one-zone (or direct-heat) cooking, spread the coals evenly across the bottom grate (see page 9). For two-zone (or indirect-heat) cooking—my approach for most recipes in this book—bank the coals on one side of the grill, creating a cooler zone on the side with no coals (see page 8). When you dump the coals from the charcoal chimney onto the grill, they'll be bright reddish orange. You'll need to wait until they're glowing embers covered with a fine, gray ash, 15 to 20 minutes longer, before you're ready to cook.

All the recipes in this book begin with one chimney full of coal. Recipes that need additional charcoal during the cooking process are noted. A hinged cooking grate is super-helpful here (the hinged side should open above the coals). If you don't have a hinged grate, you'll need a couple of pairs of sturdy tongs to carefully remove the hot grate and place it on the ground (I usually lean mine against the grill) while you add more coals. The best way to have more coals ready when you need them is to start a second fire in the chimney about the same time you put your food on the grill (be sure to place the chimney full of coals on a concrete surface, not wood).

If you're using a gas grill, check the propane level before starting and follow the manufacturer's instructions for your grill. Typically, this means lifting the lid (so unlit gas fumes don't collect in the cook box), opening the valve on the propane tank, turning the dials to the flame symbol, and then pushing the button that ignites them. Once the flames appear, turn the heat to high, close the lid, and allow the grill to heat for 10 to 15 minutes.

Step 2: Choose Your Cooking Method

There are two ways to lay a charcoal fire for cooking.

Direct cooking (hot and fast): The first approach (shown on page 9) is to spread the coals evenly over the entire bottom grate of the grill, which gives you the same level of heat wherever you place the food; this is a one-zone, or single-level, fire for direct-heat cooking. This setup is my go-to when I'm cooking pizza on a preheated stone. To create one-zone cooking with a gas grill, turn all the burners to the same level of heat and rely on the built-in thermometer to gauge temperature.

Indirect cooking (slower and moderate): The other approach for laying a fire—and by far the most versatile—is to bank the hot coals on one side of the grill and leave the other side empty to create a two-zone fire for indirect cooking (shown on page 8). This is my preference for cooking just about everything: It provides much more flexibility because the cooler "safety zone" allows you to manage heat. When you have flare-ups, for instance, you can quickly move food away from the fire (and/or close the grill to snuff out the flame), and the problem is solved. To create two levels of heat in a gas grill, simply turn off one side of the burners (or the middle burner if your grill has three). If your grill has an upper-tier warming rack, you can also use that as a cooler zone.

Step 3: Clean and Oil the Grates

To ensure foods cook evenly and don't stick to the grates and/or taste acrid and sooty, it's essential to clean the grill grates before cooking. Cleaning the grates is a three-step process.

Preheat: After you dump the hot coals from a charcoal chimney onto the lower cooking grate or turn a gas grill to high, allow the grill to preheat for 10 to 15 minutes to burn off any food residue.

Clean the hot grates: Carefully wipe the hot grates with a paper towel moistened in vegetable oil (no need for expensive extra-virgin olive oil here). The towel will wipe away a significant layer of black, sooty carbon left behind from your last meal. Next, use a stainless-steel grill brush to scrub the grates free of any remaining debris.

Oil the grates again: Use a clean paper towel to carefully oil the grates a second time. Another option? My favorite way to oil the grates comes from a tip courtesy of the competitive barbecue circuit: Spear an onion half with a two-pronged carving fork, dip the cut side into a shallow dish of vegetable oil, then rub it over the entire grate. The onion releases the oil and its steamy juices, and the fork allows you to rub more firmly and longer than you can with a paper towel.

Indirect cooking (left) is done over a cooler zone to manage heat; direct cooking (above) is done over the hottest part of the fire.

In addition to cleaning the grates, you'll also want to empty cooled ashes from your charcoal grill on a regular basis—this allows for better circulation and a "cleaner" burn (i.e., not choked with ash). For obvious reasons, you'll want to clean the cooking basin of a gas grill before you turn it on: Carefully remove the cooking grates, then use a stainless-steel grill brush to brush excess grease and debris from inside the cook box to the bottom tray, empty the tray, and wipe it clean with a moistened cloth.

Step 4: Feel the Heat

Cooking food over the right level of heat is just as important as how you lay your coals. The most effective way to gauge the heat of your fire is by using the hand test. Place your palm over the hot charcoals 5 inches (13cm) above the cooking grate. If you need to pull your hand away after 2 to 4 seconds, the heat is high. If you need to pull your hand away after 5 to 7 seconds, the heat is medium. If you need to pull your hand away after 8 to 10 seconds, the heat is low. Do this a few times and it will become an intuitive process.

- High (450°–550°F/230°–290°C): 2–4 seconds

- Medium (350°–450°F/175°–230°C): 5–7 seconds

- Low (250°–350°F/120°–175°C): 8–10 seconds

If you're using a grill pan, preheat it over medium heat for 4 to 5 minutes, until very hot (a drop of water will sizzle and quickly evaporate). Oil the pan just before cooking; otherwise it will smoke and burn.

TROUBLESHOOTING

Until you're in a regular groove, grilling can be intimidating. But it's an easy and straightforward cooking method, especially when you know a few simple tricks for keeping your cool and maintaining control over the fire. You'll find recipe-specific tips throughout the book, but here are three ways to avoid general mishaps.

Controlling Flare-Ups

Your goal is to cook over fire, not amidst flames that engulf and blacken your food. When fat drips onto hot coals (or the flame of a gas grill), it vaporizes and ignites, so flare-ups are inevitable. Luckily, there are two easy ways to manage them: The first is to always cook with a two-zone setup (see Step 2, page 7). This creates a cooler area, or a "safety zone," away from the fire where you can transfer foods when heat flares. The second way to control flare-ups is to starve them of oxygen. To do this, quickly close the grill for a few seconds and close the air intake vents—the fire should die down within seconds. Whatever you do, don't squirt the coals with a water bottle; this will stir the sooty ash from the bottom of the grill up into your food.

Avoiding Sticky Situations

When a grill is clean, hot, and oiled and whatever you're grilling is lightly coated in oil, food should not stick. As long as it's had enough time to cook, that is. Most foods will stick to a grill initially, but after they've had enough time to form a charred crust, they're easy to flip. (If you and your tongs start messing with delicate food too soon, there's a good chance you'll tear it.) If food is sticking to the grates, give it an additional minute or two of cooking time to form a crust. If you still need help, use tongs to gently lift one side of the item, then use a decisive thrust to slide a thin, slotted fish spatula underneath the food to release it from the grates.

TWO WAYS TO ADD A WHIFF OF WOODSMOKE

Charcoal burns hotter and more efficiently than wood, but a wood fire—the oldest cooking method around—imparts a distinct flavor (you know what I'm talking about if you've been seduced by the aroma of a wood-burning pizza oven). Here are two easy ways to infuse the flavor of woodsmoke to whatever you're cooking.

Wood Chips

Adding wood chips to a charcoal fire or gas grill is a great way to infuse food with an additional layer of complexity and smoky goodness. Distinctive varieties of wood (mesquite, hickory, pecan, fruitwood) impart unique nuances, though the differences can be subtle. For the shorter cooking times in this book, you'd be hard-pressed to taste the specific variety of wood. But as a general rule, use milder varieties such as hickory and fruitwood for pork and fish and the stronger flavor of mesquite for beef.

To use wood chips, soak them in water (or beer or wine, for yet another nuance) for 30 minutes. Absorbing moisture allows the wood to smolder slowly without bursting into flames. Once drained, you can scatter the chips directly onto the hot, glowing coals. I place them around the periphery so they burn slowly and don't put out the fire. For a gas grill, you can wrap the soaked chips in two layers of heavy-duty aluminum foil. Then perforate the top of the packet with a knife, leave it slightly open, or place the soaked chips in a metal smoker box that's placed directly over the heat. Specific recipes that benefit from woodsmoke are flagged throughout the book, but feel free to use wood chips for cooking pizza, pork chops, or steak, or whenever the flavor appeals.

Put a Log on It

In addition to wood chips, you can also use larger wood chunks (typically used in low-and-slow barbecue) or logs if you place them alongside your bed of hot, glowing embers. If you have access to hardwood logs, make sure they're dry and cured and not too moist and green; otherwise they'll generate a black smoke that will give food an unpleasant taste. This allows the wood to burn slowly for a longer-lasting fire, as well as add flavor to whatever you're cooking. Larger pieces of wood should not be used on a gas grill.

Cooking Through Before Blackening Crust

You've got a gorgeous browned skin but your drumsticks are still pink at the bone? This is where a two-zone fire will save you every time. If an item is blackening too quickly, move it to a milder temperature zone to finish cooking through. If you have a perfectly bronzed bird but your chicken isn't up to temperature, move it off direct heat, close the grill, vent accordingly for indirect cooking, and give it a few more minutes. The milder heat will allow the interior to cook through without getting too dark on the outside.

HANDY TOOLS

When it comes to getting weeknight dinner on the table, organization is everything. For the most part, fancy, expensive gadgets are unnecessary, but these basic tools will help you knock out dinner with a sense of ease.

Apron: Aprons protect my clothes from being ash-dusted, and ones with pockets can also hold extra matches, my phone, and my lip gloss. Loop an extra kitchen towel under the apron string, I promise you'll need it (for oily hands after you sample a charred green bean, for instance).

Cleaning brush: Use this to sweep out the cooled ashes from the cook box of a charcoal grill (and use a metal pail to collect the ashes).

Grill basket: Sometimes called a fish or vegetable basket, this is typically a square, sided pan or a hinged metal grid that allows you to cook smaller items without them slipping through the grates and/or to flip the entire basket without having to manipulate more delicate items. (I use this type of model for grilling cauliflower steaks and potato rounds.) My go-to for smaller items like shrimp and mushrooms is a stainless-steel rimmed tray that allows me to use tongs to shake the basket (as you would shake a skillet to help foods brown evenly) or stir the items as they grill.

Long-handled metal spatula: A confident shove of a metal spatula flips food while maintaining its browned crust. A spatula is also helpful in securing larger items that need more support (e.g., whole fish) when you flip them.

Long-handled tongs: They help with everything—placing food on and taking it off the grill, rearranging charcoal, and lifting the grill grate to add more charcoal. Long-handled tongs help you work over a hot fire without burning your hands; spring-loaded models give you one less thing to manipulate.

Meat thermometer: It takes the guesswork out of gauging doneness. For the most accurate results, use an instant-read digital thermometer.

Metal trash pail: These are helpful for storing and protecting charcoal, wood chunks and chips, and even paper for the charcoal chimney from the elements.

Rimmed baking sheets: Use these for transporting bowls of *mise en place*, tools, and kitchen towels to and from the grill. I also use them to transfer hot-off-the-grill items to serving dishes or to a low oven, to keep warm while I finish the rest of the meal (such as when I'm grilling a lot of wings or drumsticks for a party).

Stainless-steel grill brush: This is essential for scraping debris from the grill grates.

Wooden matches: I fiddled around with small restaurant matches a couple of times before realizing life (and lighting charcoal chimneys) is much easier with sturdy wooden kitchen matches.

WAYS TO UP YOUR GRILL GAME

Once you've mastered the basic setup, attention to a few details will help you finesse the fire, maximize flavor, and have more fun.

Embrace the Experience

That means rolling with the occasional imperfections—you'll learn from your mistakes. Relish in the fact that outdoor cooking allows you to unplug from your daily routine, engage with an interactive cooking method, and connect with your surroundings and your favorite people who gravitate to the wafting aromas of whatever you're cooking. Also, never underestimate the added benefits of a playlist and cold beverage.

Season Generously—and in Advance

When it comes to cooking meat or fish, seasoning is the first task on my prep list. For the fullest flavor, you'll want to season meat or fish generously up to an hour in advance (timing specifics are listed with each recipe), and then allow it to come to room temperature while you heat the grill and prep the rest of the meal.

Be Organized

Whether you're grilling pizzas or greens, you'll get better results and feel more confident during the process if you have everything you need (grilling tools, kitchen towels, ingredients) prepped and in place before you start cooking. Grilling is a hands-on process, and cooking times are often short. The last thing you want to do is scramble for, say, a kitchen towel when your food is over the fire.

Stay Engaged

Every fire is slightly different, and even gas grills typically have hot spots, so from the moment you place food—particularly quick-cooking items—on the hot grates, keep your tongs in hand and pay attention to the process (the sound of the sizzle, the color of the char) so you can respond accordingly. In other words, this is not the time to post on Instagram or weed potted plants—trust me on this. Managing heat to achieve the results you want—a perfectly charred juicy burger, crispy browned chicken skin—often means flipping food frequently and moving it around the heat several times during the process.

Make the Most of Your Fire

Once you're in your grilling groove, it's downright painful not to make the most of the lingering heat. Use the fire to cook something else, which will give you a jump start on flavor-packed meals for the following day or week. For instance, round out your meal or cook ahead for the week with a few quick-cooking items like grilled vegetables or bread. If your fire has gotten very low, simply remove the cooking grate and place the grill basket directly on the ash-covered coals. Or you can coal-roast onions, eggplant, or beets while you eat the dinner you've just prepared—they require very little attention. Then you'll be armed with smoky, deeply flavored ingredients to make ratatouille, grain salads, or soups the next day. Of course, you can also use the lingering heat to fire up dessert—see loads of ideas starting on page 196.

Grill Often

Just like piecrusts and biscuits, grilling requires a "feel," both for managing heat and gauging doneness, that improves with repetition. The more you grill, the better you'll become.

Let's Start with a Drink

Whether you're craving a cocktail infused with a whiff of smoke (hello, grilled satsumas) or something crisp and austere as a neutral backdrop for charred flavors, cooking over a hot fire is more fun with an adult beverage in hand. Here are a few of my favorite backyard libations. If you're grilling the components of a cocktail like citrus or pineapple, you'll want to do that first, on a clean oiled grate, so your drink doesn't taste like your dinner.

French Place 75

The first time I tasted the nectar-like perfume of St-Germain, it was from the lips of an ice luge at a friend's birthday party, but that's another story for another time. At our house on French Place (the street we live on), the elderflower liqueur adds the perfect balance to the lightly tart, fizzy classic. To make 1 drink, fill a cocktail shaker with 1½ ounces gin, ½ ounce St-Germain, 1 ounce fresh lemon juice, and 2 dashes grapefruit bitters with a scoop of ice. Shake vigorously, strain into a vintage coupe glass, top with a splash of champagne or dry sparkling wine, and garnish with a twist of lemon peel. *Good with Creamy Kale Toasts (page 24) and Herb-Basted Smoked Salmon (page 122).*

My Perfect G&T

Start with the right glass, a super-thin delicate whiskey glass that makes the botanical notes in gin pop. Trust me, this is an entirely different drink in a chunky glass. To make 1 cocktail, fill the glass three-quarters full with ice cubes, add 1½ ounces Plymouth Gin, a swath of grapefruit peel, a rosemary sprig (thyme or sage are also nice when you want to mix it up), and top with Fever-Tree tonic water. Stir 6 to 8 revolutions, imagine the world as you'd like it to be, and sip. Repeat as needed, but start from scratch (no secondhand ice!). *Good as an aperitif with an unfolding fire, Crackly Rosemary Flatbread (page 28), and Grilled Branzino with Thai Basil Butter (page 127).*

Sparkling Yuzu Lemongrass Lemonade

This grown-up lemonade will get you through the most sweltering months of summer. To make the lemongrass simple syrup, in a small saucepan combine 1 cup (240ml) water, 1 cup (200g) unrefined cane sugar, and 1 lemongrass stalk (bottom trimmed, outer layers removed, thinly sliced). Bring to a boil, stirring to dissolve sugar, over medium-high heat; set aside to cool and steep for 20 to 30 minutes. Strain syrup, discard lemongrass, and refrigerate for up to 2 weeks. To make 1 cocktail, combine 2 ounces (60ml) vodka, 1 ounce lemongrass simple syrup, 1 ounce fresh tangerine juice, and ½ ounce yuzu juice in a cocktail shaker. Add enough ice to fill the shaker halfway, close the top, and shake vigorously until very cold. Fill a tall glass with ice cubes and slices of tangerine, strain cocktail into glass, and top off with Topo Chico or ginger beer. *Good with Salt-Crusted Snapper (page 130) and Charred Steak Tips with Asian Herb Salad (page 190).*

The Lower East Side

The smoked salmon and bialy mecca that is Russ & Daughters (on Orchard Street in New York) also serves seriously refined cocktails like this bracing dill-and-cucumber-perfumed elixir. To make 1 drink, muddle 3 slices of cucumber in a cocktail shaker. Add a scoop of ice, ¾ ounce fresh lime juice, ¾ ounce simple syrup, 2 ounces (60ml) Tanqueray (or another London-dry-style gin), and a pinch of fresh dill fronds, and shake vigorously until very cold. Double-strain the cocktail into a chilled coupe (or martini) glass and garnish with 1 small, feathery dill sprig. *Good with Crackly Rosemary Flatbread (page 28) and smoked salmon, horseradish cream, and fresh dill; Chicories with Charred Scallion Dressing (page 64); and Basic Grilled Fish with Grilled Vegetable Vinaigrette (page 112).*

Diego's Paloma

Cuidado: The lip-tingling heat of chile salt, a brazen pour of tequila, and a splash of fizzy grapefruit soda create a potent, wildly refreshing elixir. For 1 cocktail, make chile salt by combining 3 tablespoons pure ground chile pepper (such as New Mexico), 1 tablespoon sugar, and 1 tablespoon kosher salt in a shallow bowl. Use a lime wedge to wet the rim of a highball glass and dip the rim in the chile salt to coat. Carefully fill the glass with ice and add 2 ounces (60ml) tequila blanco, ½ ounce fresh lime juice, a splash of grapefruit soda, and a swath of grapefruit peel. Top off the drink with Topo Chico (or another sparkling water with assertive bubbles that makes your eyes water) and stir. *Good with Grill-Roasted Chicken with Tomatillo Salsa (page 151) and Skirt Steak with Salsa Verde (page 189).*

Grilled Satsuma Margarita

A kiss of heat adds a caramelized depth to this sultry riff. To make 1 cocktail, halve 2 satsumas (or blood oranges or tangerines) horizontally and grill them cut side down on clean oiled grates over medium heat until nice grill marks appear. Fill a cocktail shaker with 1½ ounces grilled satsuma juice, 2 ounces (60ml) mezcal, ½ ounce Cointreau, and ½ ounce fresh lime juice, shake vigorously, and strain over fresh ice. Garnish with a lime slice. *Good with Grilled Corn Nachos (page 91) and Gulf Coast Shrimp Tacos (page 121).*

Boulevardier

Made with rye whiskey instead of gin and dating back to the 1920s, a Boulevardier is the Negroni's voluptuous cousin. I like to use a sweet vermouth that leans toward amaro, with stronger bittersweet herbal notes, like Punt e Mes. To make 1 cocktail, chill a coupe or rocks glass in the freezer. Pour 1½ ounces rye whiskey, 1 ounce Punt e Mes, and 1 ounce Campari into a cocktail shaker or mixing glass, add a handful of ice, and stir until chilled. Strain into the chilled glass and garnish with a swath of orange peel. *Good with Straight-Up Lamb Burgers (page 174) and Rebel Tomahawk (page 193).*

Chip's Baltimore Glider

My friend Chip Wass has a wild talent for choosing just the right cocktail for any setting. For instance, the signature drink on his leafy back patio in Baltimore is this exceptionally smooth, amiable blend of American whiskey balanced with the tartness of lemon and the sweetness of black currant liqueur. To make 1 drink, combine 2 ounces (60ml) bourbon, 1 ounce fresh lemon juice, ½ ounce crème de cassis, ½ ounce simple syrup, a few dashes of Angostura bitters, and a scoop of ice in a cocktail shaker and shake vigorously. Strain into an ice-filled old-fashioned glass and garnish with a lemon slice or, if in season, fresh black currants. *Good with State Park Potatoes (page 51) and Sweet & Smoky Drumsticks (page 143).*

Grilled Pineapple Punch

The smoky-sweet notes of grilled pineapple meld dangerously with dark rum. To make about 8 drinks, cut a peeled cored pineapple lengthwise into spears about 1½ inches (4cm) wide. Grill them over medium heat until charred on both sides, 8 to 10 minutes, and set aside. In a large pitcher, combine 2½ cups (590ml) dark rum, 1 cup (240ml) pineapple juice, ½ cup (120ml) ginger liqueur (e.g., Barrow's Intense Ginger Liqueur), 1½ to 2 ounces (45 to 60ml) fresh lime juice, a cinnamon stick, and a split vanilla bean. Slide the pineapple spears onto pretty bamboo (or other) skewers, place them in the pitcher, and refrigerate until ready to serve. Before serving, add ice to the pitcher and place one skewer inside each tall glass. *Good with Seafood Paella with Freekeh & Lima Beans (page 135) and Party Wings with Cholula Butter (page 138).*

Dough

GRILLED BREAD, A LOVE STORY

As a baker's wife, I'm accustomed to making the most of day-old loaves. My husband, David Norman, has been baking bread for more than thirty years. We met when we were living in New York, and when he finished the night shift at Bouley Bakery, sometimes he'd walk across the Brooklyn Bridge to my apartment in the Heights to deliver a freshly baked loaf (I know, right?). These days, he's the head baker (or dough puncher, as he likes to say) and partner at Easy Tiger Bake Shop & Beer Garden in Austin. Although I'm certainly biased, his mad talent with flour, water, and yeast creates the sort of deeply flavored loaves that send people on Proustian journeys of giddy reflection. Needless to say, the cinematic version of our life together might be called *It's a Wonderful Loaf.*

On most days, our "bread basket" (a painted wooden trough we purchased in Nuevo Laredo, Mexico, just across the Texas border) is an embarrassment of riches—piled with baguettes, crusty rounds of levain and sourdough, and dense, hearty loaves of walnut bread and rye.

While a bread basket can be forgettable, a platter of warm, fragrant slices of grilled bread makes its presence known. Rubbed while still warm with garlic (the ragged edges of the toasted bread release the aroma of the garlic's fragrant oil), covered with a generous drizzle of your best extra-virgin olive oil (it should seep from the bread and pool on the plate), and finished with a sprinkle of flaky salt, it's a sensual pleasure that surpasses the sum of its elemental parts.

When the rest of our pantry is mostly bare, the kids are "starving," and we're too tired to rustle up anything elaborate, I know I can make a quick and incredibly satisfying picnic dinner, as we call it, by pulling out bits and pieces (half wedges of cheese, olives, charcuterie, marinated and pickled vegetables), slicing up a day-old loaf, and firing up the grill. The mix-and-match results are, truthfully, among my favorite dinners.

When we're looking for something warm and welcoming (and easy) for guests to munch on while gathering around the fire, we'll serve grilled bread—a vehicle for whatever we have on hand, such as tapenade, luscious white bean puree, chèvre, avocado, butter and shaved watermelon radishes, or simply a scattering of fresh herbs. And when dinner is missing something to pull the other components together—meat drippings, creamy sauce, vinaigrette—grilled bread makes the meal (see ideas on page 23).

How to Grill Bread

Start with sturdy loaf of day-old artisan bread. It has less moisture than a just-baked loaf, so it will toast better, and its flavor will be intensified by the heat of the fire. Also, anytime you reheat stale bread it actually reverses the staling process (caused by a change in the starch structure, called starch retrogradation) for a short time. Plus, it kills my husband when I toast a fresh loaf of bread. I love levain or miche, but any rustic or hearty country-style loaf that can hold its own against a char will work just fine. Cut the bread into 1/2-inch (1.3cm) slices, place them over a medium fire, and use tongs to flip the bread when grill marks appear and the bread is toasted, about 1 minute on each side. Swipe a halved clove of garlic, cut side down, over the top of the bread, drizzle with your best extra-virgin olive oil, and sprinkle with flaky salt, a few grinds of pepper, and a few fresh herbs (small whole leaves or chiffonade), if desired.

Leftover Grilled Bread = Grilled Bread Crumbs

If you're lucky enough to have leftover slices of grilled bread, use them to make grilled bread crumbs, which will make any number of dishes more delicious. (In fact, you might just want to plan ahead and grill a few extra slices; wrap them in foil after they cool.) Break or crumble a few pieces of grilled bread into a food processor and process into a coarse mixture—don't worry about making the crumbs uniform. At this point, simply moisten the crumbs with olive oil and season with salt and pepper, or flavor them with just about anything, including anchovies, fresh herbs, olives, sesame seeds, crumbled nori, gochugaru (Korean red pepper flakes), or toasted nuts. Use grilled bread crumbs as a topping for pasta, any grilled or roasted vegetable, salads, or scrambled eggs. Unflavored bread crumbs can be stored in an airtight container for 3 or 4 days; flavored bread crumbs should be used immediately or stored in the fridge for 1 day.

Texas Toast

Grilled bread typically suggests a rustic loaf, but I also love to toast thick slabs of—ideally day-old—*pain de mic*, or any white bread that's enriched with butter and eggs (such as brioche), to make Texas toast. These breads brown faster than rustic varieties, so watch them closely and keep your tongs in hand. With a lightly golden crust and a tender, chewy middle, they make a crispy, comforting base for soft-boiled eggs, leftover brisket and barbecue sauce, Sunday's chuck roast, a scoop of tuna or chicken salad, or smashed avocados and chile flakes. The kids love it with a smear of Nutella or, every now and then, marshmallow cream and sprinkles.

GRILLED BREAD TOPPINGS THAT MAKE A MEAL

When crowded with a couple well-chosen ingredients, sidekick toasts become your next favorite lunch, dinner, or hearty snack.

- SOFTENED BUTTER + JUICE FROM A GRILLED LEMON + HERB-BASTED SMOKED SALMON (PAGE 122)

- OLIVE TAPENADE + GRILLED EGGPLANT + FRESH MOZZARELLA

- FETA (PUREED WITH OLIVE OIL AND RED PEPPER FLAKES) + GRILLED RIBBONS OF CROOKNECK SQUASH + SMALL FRESH MINT LEAVES

- KEWPIE MAYO + SHAVED PARMESAN + GRILLED MACKEREL + THINLY SLICED SERRANO

- HUMMUS + RINGS OF PICKLED PEPPERS + MICROGREENS

- CHOPPED CHICKEN + GRILLED LEMON MAYO (PAGE 81)

- SLICED POTATOES + DILL MAYO + PICKLED RED ONIONS (PAGE 176)

Creamy Kale Toasts

Makes enough for 8 toasts, with leftovers

1 cup (240ml) full-fat Greek yogurt

3 tablespoons extra-virgin olive oil, plus more for drizzling

2 teaspoons fresh lemon juice

1 teaspoon finely grated lemon zest

Pinch of red pepper flakes

Kosher salt and freshly ground black pepper

½ cup (50g) grated aged goat cheese (such as Cypress Grove Midnight Moon)

1 bunch lacinato kale (12 ounces/340g)

8 thick slices levain or another rustic Italian bread

1 clove garlic, halved lengthwise

Flaky salt

Grilling stems of kale and other sturdy greens is a quick, easy process that dramatically transforms their taste and texture. The leaves won't char evenly, and that's fine—you want a mix of doneness that ranges from blackened and crackly to deep green and tender. The smoky flavor of this luscious spread intensifies overnight—the depth of flavor will surprise and delight you—so you'll be happy to have leftovers to slather on bagels or toasted walnut bread. This spread can also be made with other greens (collards, mustard, turnip) and other leftover vegetables (grilled and finely chopped fennel, celery, carrots). Don't wash the kale unless you absolutely must—it crisps much better if the leaves are completely dry.

1. Prepare a charcoal grill for two-zone cooking and build a medium fire, or heat a gas grill to medium-high. Carefully wipe the preheated grill grates with a lightly oiled paper towel. Using a grill brush, scrape the grill grates clean, then carefully wipe with a lightly oiled towel again.

2. In a large bowl, combine the yogurt with the olive oil, lemon juice and zest, and red pepper flakes. Season with kosher salt and pepper and then fold in the cheese.

3. Working in batches, grill the kale leaves perpendicular to the grates so they won't fall through. Cook over direct heat until lightly charred, 1 to 2 minutes on each side. Transfer to a cutting board and cool slightly. Use a knife to trim the thick ribs from each leaf and then finely chop the kale leaves. Fold into the yogurt mixture.

4. Grill the bread over direct heat until charred, about a minute on each side. While still warm, rub 1 side of each toast with the cut side of the garlic. Top each toast with a slather of the creamy kale and arrange the toasts on a platter. Drizzle with olive oil and sprinkle with flaky salt.

Crackly Rosemary Flatbread

Makes six 10-inch (25cm) rounds

3½ cups (440g)
unbleached
all-purpose flour

2 tablespoons freshly
chopped rosemary plus
2 sprigs

2 teaspoons baking
powder

1½ teaspoons kosher salt

1 cup (240ml) water

⅔ cup (160ml) olive oil,
plus more for brushing

Flaky salt (optional)

Toppings of choice
(see opposite for ideas)

For years my friend Molly Meloy has had this theory that the most blissful stretch of each day is the golden evening hours between four and seven. I fully agree, because it plays to my sipping and snacking proclivities. My ideal combination for a predinner graze is a cracker-like flatbread served with a few creamy and piquant toppings, such as tapenade, hummus, Smoky Eggplant Dip (page 82), and vegetable relishes. This recipe, adapted from one that appeared in an issue of *Gourmet*, can be changed up in countless ways—use thyme, oregano, parsley, or tarragon (or a combination), or add heat with toasted crushed peppercorns or crumbled dried chiles, fennel or cumin seeds, or spices. Once you make the dough, this flatbread is easy to knock out while you're chatting with friends by the fire, as it cooks in just a few minutes.

1. In a medium bowl, whisk together the flour, chopped rosemary, baking powder, and kosher salt. Make a well in center, then add the water and oil and gradually stir into the flour with a wooden spoon until a dough forms. Transfer the dough to a work surface (you won't need additional flour) and knead gently 4 or 5 times until you have a smooth, supple round. Cover the dough with a clean kitchen towel and let rest for 15 to 20 minutes. Knead again, re-cover with the towel, and let rest for an additional 15 to 20 minutes.

2. Prepare a charcoal grill for one-zone cooking and build a medium-high fire, or heat a gas grill to high. Carefully wipe the preheated grill grates with a lightly oiled paper towel. Using a grill brush, scrape the grill grates clean, then carefully wipe with a lightly oiled towel again.

3. Divide dough into 6 pieces and cover with a kitchen towel. On a lightly floured surface, roll out 1 piece of dough into a rustic 6- to 7-inch (15 to 18cm) round. Let the dough rest for a few minutes and then continue to roll into a 9- to 10-inch (23 to 25cm) round that's about ¼ inch (6mm) thick. Lightly brush the top with oil and lightly press small clusters of fresh rosemary leaves on top. Use your hands to drape the dough onto the hot grates (quickly reshaping the round if it has lost its shape), close the grill, and cook until lightly charred on the bottom, 1 to 2 minutes. Use tongs and your fingers to flip the flatbread, close the grill, and cook until charred and browned in spots, an additional minute or two. Transfer the flatbread to a rack to cool and finish with flaky salt, if desired. Repeat with the remaining rounds.

4. Break the flatbread into large shards or slather a round with your desired toppings. Store in an airtight container at room temperature for up to 2 days.

A FEW FAVORITE FLATBREAD TOPPINGS

If I'm not using flatbread as a scoop, I like to slather the entire round or large shards with toppings. Here are a few favorite combinations.

- GREEN OLIVE TAPENADE + FRESH OREGANO LEAVES

- SMALL BOILED SHRIMP + QUARK + SHAVED FENNEL AND FENNEL FRONDS (OR SHAVED RADISHES)

- SMOKED SALMON + HORSERADISH CREAM + CHOPPED FRESH DILL

- LABNEH + SPICED SEED CRUNCH (SEE BELOW)

Spiced Seed Crunch

Sugar, a whiff of warm spices, and egg white transform a pretty mix of seeds into crunchy, addictive brittle that's delicious as a topping for yogurt, creamy purees (like beet hummus), salads—and, no doubt, grilled flatbread. Heat the oven to 300°F (150°C) and line a rimmed baking sheet with parchment paper. In a bowl, whisk together 1 egg white, 3 tablespoons turbinado sugar, ½ teaspoon ras el hanout, ½ teaspoon kosher salt, and a pinch of cayenne. Add ¼ cup (50g) millet, ¼ cup (35g) black sesame seeds, and ¼ cup (35g) pumpkin seeds and toss to coat. Transfer mixture to baking sheet, letting excess egg white drip back into the bowl. Bake, tossing occasionally, until mixture is golden brown and fragrant, 15 to 20 minutes. Let cool. Store in an airtight container at room temperature for up to 1 week.

Crispy Greek Pies with Dandelion & Feta

Makes about 12 pies

Phyllo Dough

3 cups (375g)
all-purpose flour

1 teaspoon kosher salt

½ cup (120ml) cold
water, plus more as
needed

¼ cup (60ml) olive oil,
plus more for brushing

1½ tablespoons white
wine vinegar

Cornstarch or rice flour,
for dusting

Filling

2 bunches (about
12 ounces/340g)
dandelion greens, ends
and thick stems trimmed
(or any combination of
spinach, mustard, or
other cooking greens)

Kosher salt

1 cup (150g) crumbled
feta cheese, or ¾ cup
(75g) grated Pecorino
Romano or Asiago mixed
with 3 tablespoons
Greek yogurt

1 cup (40g) freshly
chopped parsley

½ cup (25g) freshly
chopped dill

1 teaspoon dried Greek
oregano

Pinch of red pepper
flakes (such as piquín)

Freshly ground black
pepper

A savory pie packed with a mess of greens and sharp cheese is one of my favorite things in the world to eat. Naturally, I was quick to fire up the grill when I stumbled upon a version of this recipe in *Mediterranean Vegetarian Feasts* by Greek cookbook author Aglaia Kremezi. I'll admit that making her dough was daunting, but trust me, with a little patience it rolls out into thin, supple sheets that are surprisingly easy to work with and cook into a delicate, crackly crust.

1. To make the phyllo dough, combine the flour and salt in the bowl of a stand mixer fitted with a dough hook. Add the cold water, olive oil, and vinegar. Mix at medium speed for about 5 minutes to obtain a smooth, soft dough. If the dough seems dry, add up to 3 tablespoons more water. Cover the bowl with plastic wrap and let rest for 15 minutes.

2. Meanwhile, to make the filling, blanch the greens in generously salted boiling water for 30 seconds. Drain, rinse with cool water, squeeze dry, and chop fine. Combine the chopped greens, feta, parsley, dill, oregano, and red pepper flakes with a fork. Season with salt and black pepper to taste.

3. Give the dough a quick knead and divide into 6 pieces. Dust the dough with cornstarch, then roll each piece of dough as thinly as possible, gradually stretching it into a 16-inch (40cm) round. The trick to getting the dough to continue to stretch is to give it a few seconds of rest after every 3 or 4 rolls. Cut each round in half, dust with cornstarch, and stack off to the side.

4. Prepare a charcoal grill for two-zone cooking and build a medium-high fire, or heat a gas grill or ridged grill pan to high. Carefully wipe the preheated grill grates with a lightly oiled paper towel. Using a grill brush, scrape the grill grates clean, then wipe with a lightly oiled towel again.

5. While the grill heats, assemble the pies. For each pie, lay 1 half-round phyllo on your work surface and brush with olive oil. Cover half the circle with about ¼ cup (60ml) filling. Fold the other side over and press down to seal the pie. It will be an imperfect, flat triangle with crimped edges. Repeat with the remaining dough and filling, placing finished triangles on a parchment-lined baking sheet kept in a cool place.

6. Brush the top and bottom of a pie with olive oil and cook over direct heat until golden and crisp (lowering the heat as necessary), 3 to 4 minutes. Flip and cook the other side the same way. Repeat with the remaining triangles. Serve right away, or wrap in foil and store at room temperature for a day or refrigerate for 2 to 3 days.

Pizza Dough & Inspired Pies

Makes six 10-inch (25cm) pizzas

6 cups (750g)
unbleached
all-purpose flour

¼ cup (30g) whole
wheat or rye flour

1 tablespoon kosher salt

¾ teaspoon instant yeast

2½ cups (590ml) water

2 tablespoons olive oil

1 tablespoon barley
malt syrup

Toppings of choice,
including extra-virgin
olive oil and flaky salt
(see page 36 for ideas)

I played with several doughs before falling for this one, a variation on the stellar crust that Nancy Silverton created for Mozza in Los Angeles. Made from a combination of flours with just a touch of sweetness, it's easy to work with and bakes into a chewy, crackly crust with plenty of character. I prefer to make the dough the night before and allow it to rise overnight in the fridge, because a longer, slower fermentation develops complex flavor. With the long overnight bulk ferment, you don't need to proof the dough at room temperature before grilling (bonus: colder dough is easier to wrangle).

Then, an hour before grilling, I fire up the grill, divide the dough into six rounds, and allow them to rest while I prep the toppings and make a salad. Before you start the pizza train (meaning drape the first crust over the grates), make sure that all hands are on deck and toppings are ready to roll. Grilled pizzas aren't complicated, but they come together quickly, so the process is infinitely smoother if you're super organized. Once those details are in place, you're free to uncork a bottle of wine, focus on achieving perfectly charred crust, and enjoy the process—which is a lot of fun.

1. Combine both flours, the kosher salt, yeast, water, olive oil, and barley malt syrup in the bowl of a stand mixer fitted with a dough hook. Mix at low speed for about 8 minutes, until the dough begins to form a ball and pull away from the bowl. Cover the bowl with a kitchen towel and let rest for 20 minutes.

2. Turn the dough onto a lightly floured work surface and shape into a rustic square about ¼ inch (6mm) thick. Stretch and fold a flap from 1 corner into the middle, followed by the opposite corner, pushing them into the dough, then repeat with the 2 remaining corners. Return the dough to the bowl, cover, and let rest for another 30 minutes. Turn the dough onto a lightly floured work surface and fold again, as you did the first time. Place the dough in an oiled bowl, cover with plastic wrap, and refrigerate overnight.

3. About 1 hour before grilling (or the morning before you plan to cook) remove the dough from the fridge and turn it onto a lightly floured work surface. Divide the dough into 6 even-ish rounds. Tuck the edges of each round of dough under itself to form a tight ball. Place the rounds on a greased baking sheet, cover with plastic wrap, and refrigerate for at least 1 hour (or up to 12 hours) to allow the gluten to relax.

CONTINUED

4. While you rest the dough, prepare your toppings and create a "pizza station" that includes everything you'll need to finish the pies, including extra-virgin olive oil and flaky salt. About 45 minutes before grilling, prepare a charcoal grill for one-zone cooking and build a high fire, or heat a gas grill to high, until the temperature reaches about 600°F (315°C). Carefully wipe the preheated grill grates with a lightly oiled paper towel. Using a grill brush, scrape the grill grates clean, then carefully wipe with a lightly oiled towel again.

5. When the dough is ready, generously flour your work surface with all-purpose flour and place 1 round of dough in the center. Dust the dough lightly with flour. Using your fingertips, gently tap the center of the dough to flatten it slightly. Pick up the dough, ball both fists, and with your fists facing your body, place the top edge of the dough on your fists so the round stretches downward against the backs of your hands, away from them. Move the circle of dough around your fists like the hands of a clock so the dough continues to stretch downward into a circle. When the dough has stretched to about 10 inches (25cm) in diameter, drape it over the preheated grill grates (quickly reshape the pizza if it has lost its shape) and grill 1 to 2 minutes uncovered (cover if using a gas grill), or until the bottom side is crisp and marked. Remove the crust from the grill and place it, ungrilled side down, onto a lightly oiled baking sheet. Repeat with the remaining dough rounds (closing the grill and allowing it to reheat to 450°F to 500°F/230°C to 206°C between pies). Then, when you're ready to assemble the pies, top the grilled side of each crust pizza with the desired toppings and return to the grill. Cook 3 to 5 minutes, covered, or until the toppings are cooked and the cheese is melted.

6. When the pizza is done, slide tongs and/or a big spatula under the crust and transfer it to a cutting board. Let the pizza cool for a couple of minutes, then use a chef's knife or pizza cutter to cut into wedges (4, 6, or 8) as desired.

Using a Pizza Stone

If you prefer to use a stone, you'll want to preheat it after you spread out your coals (or while you're preheating a gas grill) and stretch each crust just before assembly. Then place the round of dough on a peel dusted with flour or cornmeal, add toppings, gently slide the pizza onto stone, close the grill, and cook until the crust is blistered and crisp and the cheese has melted, 4 to 6 minutes.

Favorite Pizza Combinations

At our house, pizzas are personal affairs linked to memories of stellar pies, small villages in Tuscany, and pizza joints we've known and loved. Here are just some:

La Napoule

Spread a thin layer of Smoky Ratatouille (page 96) over the crust and top with crumbled chèvre and a scattering of olives (Niçoise or oil-cured). After cooking, garnish with fresh basil or parsley leaves.

French Place Special

Top the crust with marinated anchovies, slices of fresh mozzarella, red pepper flakes, and room-temperature kale that's been lightly sautéed in olive oil with garlic.

El Rancho

Top the crust with shaved zucchini (ribbons or rounds, neatly lined up and slightly overlapping), spoonfuls of fresh ricotta, grated Parmesan, and chopped fresh mint.

Vieux Nice

Brush the crust with a thin layer of harissa moistened with olive oil. Thinly slice uncooked potatoes on a mandoline and fan them over the harissa. Top with finely chopped pistachios and bake until the potatoes are tender. Garnish with chopped fresh parsley, mint, and tarragon.

Campo de Fiori

Spread a thin layer of fresh ricotta over the crust, top with thin slices of prosciutto cotto or speck, fan young asparagus spears or ribbons over the top, and cook until the asparagus is tender.

Feisty Goat

Top the crust with halved cherry tomatoes (ideally a mix of colors), thin rounds of serrano chile, crumbled chèvre, and chopped fresh thyme. Cook until the tomatoes have softened and released some of their juices, then drizzle with olive oil and sprinkle with flaky salt before serving.

Tarte Flambée (aka Alsatian pizza)

Makes four 10-inch (25cm) pizzas

4 rounds Pizza Dough
(page 32)

2 cups (475ml) fromage
blanc

1 cup (240ml) crème
fraîche

2 teaspoons kosher salt

½ teaspoon freshly
ground black pepper

Finely grated zest of
2 lemons

⅛ teaspoon freshly
grated nutmeg

Olive oil, for brushing

2 red onions, thinly sliced

8 ounces (225g) thick-
sliced smoked bacon, cut
crosswise into thin strips

Red pepper flakes

Some version of this easy-to-love bacon and onion pizza has been a constant thread in my food history. I've enjoyed it as a bar snack in France, prepared it for happy guests on the ranch, and my husband, David, does a version at Easy Tiger to pair with Alsatian wines. Known as *flammekueche* in Alsatian and *flammkuchen* in German, tarte flambée is the simple, satisfying confluence of thin, crispy dough; a fresh, creamy cheese (such as fromage blanc or quark); onion; and smoked bacon. The elements are straightforward but benefit from a few aromatics and attention to detail, so I decided this pie warranted its own recipe. Serve the hot, crispy wedges (or squares) with cold Alsatian wine and a frisée salad with Dijon vinaigrette. Note that this recipe makes four pizzas, so you can double-wrap the two remaining rounds of dough and freeze for another time (thawed, stretched, dimpled, and topped with olive oil, fresh herbs, and flaky salt, it makes great focaccia). Or increase the amount of cheese topping as desired to make six—you'll be happy to have leftovers.

1. An hour before grilling (or the morning before you plan to cook), remove the pizza dough from the fridge and turn it onto a lightly floured work surface. Divide the dough into 6 even-ish segments. Tuck the edges of each round of dough under itself to form a tight ball. Place the rounds on a greased baking sheet, cover with plastic, and refrigerate for another hour (or up to 12 hours) to allow the gluten to relax.

2. Meanwhile, make the cheese topping: Combine the fromage blanc, crème fraîche, salt, pepper, lemon zest, and nutmeg in a bowl; set aside (this can be prepared and refrigerated up to a day in advance).

3. Forty-five minutes before cooking, prepare a grill for one-zone cooking and build a hot fire in a charcoal grill (or heat a gas grill to high, until the temperature reaches about 600°F/315°C). Carefully wipe the preheated grates with a lightly oiled paper towel. Using a grill brush, scrape the grill grates clean, then carefully wipe with a lightly oiled towel again.

4. When your dough is ready, generously flour your work surface and place 1 round of dough in the center of the floured surface. Dust the dough lightly with flour. Using your fingertips, gently tap the center of the dough to flatten it slightly.

CONTINUED

5. Pick up the dough, ball both fists, and with your fists facing your body, place the top edge of the dough on your fists so the round stretches downward against the backs of your hands, away from them. Move the circle of dough around your fists like the hands of a clock so the dough continues to stretch downward into a circle.

6. When the dough has stretched to about 10 inches (25cm) in diameter (absolutely no need for a perfect circle here), drape it over the preheated grill grates (quickly reshape the pizza if it has lost its shape) and grill 1 to 2 minutes uncovered (cover if using a gas grill), or until the bottom side is crisp and marked. Remove crust from grill and place it, ungrilled side down, onto a lightly oiled baking sheet. Repeat with the remaining dough rounds (closing the grill and allowing it to reheat to 450°F to 500°F/230°C to 260°C between pies).

7. Then when you're ready to assemble, spread a thin layer (about ½ cup/120ml) of the cheese mixture over the grilled side of dough, leaving a ½-inch (1.3cm) border around edge. Top with a light scattering of the onions, bacon, and red pepper flakes and return to grill. Cook 3 to 5 minutes, covered, or until crisp and the onions have lightly charred. Repeat with the remaining crusts.

8. When the pizza is done, slide tongs and/or a big spatula under the crust and transfer it from the grill to a cutting board or round. Allow the pizza to cool for a couple minutes, then use a chef's knife or pizza cutter to cut into wedges (4, 6, or 8) as desired.

Cheese

Halloumi with Blood Oranges, Green Olives & Pistachios

Serves 2

2 blood oranges

3 tablespoons olive oil, plus more for brushing

2 tablespoons white wine vinegar

2 tablespoons freshly chopped oregano or mint

Kosher salt and freshly ground black pepper

6 to 8 ounces (170 to 225g) halloumi, cut into ¼-inch (6mm) slices

A couple handfuls arugula

½ cup (70g) green olives, pitted and halved

3 tablespoons toasted pistachios, chopped

Halloumi is a brined cheese from Cyprus that's traditionally made from sheep's or goat's milk. Its dense texture and low moisture content make it the perfect candidate for grilling or panfrying. The process is quick and fun to watch: As the surface of the cheese browns, the slices yield and soften slightly but retain their shape. Halloumi's salty, tangy flavor melds beautifully with the bright sweetness of citrus like blood oranges (another Cypriot staple). Served atop peppery greens with a scattering of olives and crunchy pistachios, this combination makes a casual and striking meal to serve alongside grilled bread and fresh figs. If you have leftover Smoked Beets (page 90) or roasted beets, they'd be a happy addition to this salad.

1. Prepare a charcoal grill for two-zone cooking and build a medium-high fire, or heat a gas grill to high. Carefully wipe the preheated grates with a lightly oiled paper towel. Using a grill brush, scrape the grill grates clean, then carefully wipe with a lightly oiled towel again. If you're using a grill basket, allow it to heat for 10 minutes before cooking.

2. Use a knife to trim the peels and pith from the oranges, and then slice the oranges into ½-inch (1.3cm) rounds. Squeeze the juice from the orange trimmings into a bowl and add the olive oil, vinegar, and oregano. Season with salt and pepper and whisk to blend.

3. Oil the grates or grill basket and brush the halloumi and orange slices with olive oil. Grill over direct heat until grill marks appear, 2 to 3 minutes on each side. Be sure to use a spatula or tongs to loosen the halloumi from the grates so you retain the flavorful browned crust.

4. Place the arugula on a serving platter and top with the warm halloumi and orange slices. Scatter with olives and pistachios, and drizzle with the herb vinaigrette.

Paneer & Vegetable Kebabs with Spicy Cilantro Oil

Serves 4

1 bunch cilantro (leaves and tender stems)

1 serrano chile, stemmed and seeded

1 clove garlic, crushed and sliced

½ teaspoon ground coriander

½ cup (120ml) olive oil, plus more for brushing

Kosher salt and freshly ground black pepper

8 to 10 ounces (225 to 285g) paneer cheese, cut into 1-inch (2.5cm) cubes

1 Japanese eggplant, cut into 1-inch (2.5cm) cubes

2 small zucchini, cut into 1-inch (2.5cm) cubes

1 cup (150g) yellow or red cherry tomatoes

Naan or pita

Lemon wedges

This recipe liberates paneer from its traditional role in Indian cuisine as partner to spinach in *saag paneer* via skewers of fresh vegetables and bright, spicy herb-chile marinade. Paneer is a mild, fresh cheese with an appealing tofu-like texture (feel free to use that instead). Slicing the cheese and vegetables into a similar size will help them cook evenly.

1. Puree the cilantro, serrano, garlic, coriander, and olive oil in a blender until smooth. Season with salt and pepper and give it another whirl. Place the paneer in a bowl and pour half of the cilantro oil over the cheese; stir to combine and then marinate in the fridge for 1 hour or up to 1 day. Set the remaining oil aside (or refrigerate it if cooking the following day).

2. Thirty minutes before cooking, soak 8 to 10 wooden skewers in water. Prepare a charcoal grill for two-zone cooking and build a medium-high fire, or heat a gas grill to high. Carefully wipe the preheated grill grates with a lightly oiled paper towel. Using a grill brush, scrape the grill grates clean, then carefully wipe with a lightly oiled towel again. Skewer the cheese, eggplant, zucchini, and cherry tomatoes as you please and grill over direct heat until the vegetables char and edges of the paneer become golden brown, 4 to 5 minutes on both sides, brushing with additional marinade from the cheese bowl. Season the kebabs with a sprinkle of salt. Brush each round of naan with olive oil and grill until charred and crisp, about 1 to 2 minutes on each side.

3. Serve kebabs with the grilled naan, lemon wedges, and the reserved marinade.

Grilling with Flavored Oils

Flavored oils made by blending oil with fresh herbs, aromatics (garlic, ginger, chile peppers), and/or spices (harissa, curry powder) provide an easy way to make grilled foods even more enticing. You'll want to use flavored oils to marinate milder, denser proteins—like cheese, firm tofu, chicken breasts, and fish fillets—before grilling so they have time (even 30 minutes) to infuse the ingredient. Brushing on additional oil during or after grilling maximizes flavor even more; if you're grilling meat or fish, reserve a portion of the oil to brush on after cooking so there's no risk of cross contamination. By contrast, vegetables benefit from a fragrant oil or dressing after grilling because the high heat creates a crust that helps retain their texture and distinct taste.

Queso Panela Tacos with Zucchini & Sweet Corn

Serves 4

2 zucchini, yellow crookneck squash, or Mexican squash (called calabacita or tatuma), halved lengthwise

2 ears corn, shucked

1 pound (450g) panela or asadero cheese, cut into ½-inch (1.3cm) slices

Olive oil

3 tablespoons freshly chopped cilantro (leaves and tender stems)

½ teaspoon dried Mexican oregano, crumbled

2 teaspoons fresh lime juice, plus more as desired

Kosher salt

8 to 10 corn tortillas

Tomatillo Salsa (optional; page 151)

Panela is semisoft Mexican cheese that's often served crumbed over salads. But don't limit its subtly sweet, milky goodness to a garnish—crispy, gooey grilled panela is the stuff that taco dreams are made of. After grilling, you can nestle the cheese slices in a pool of Tomatillo Salsa (page 151) that's easy to assemble beforehand (or a day in advance), or serve them simply in warm corn tortillas with a mixture of charred zucchini, sweet corn, sautéed kale, spinach, or grilled mushrooms. You can also serve grilled panela "fajita style" with a sizzling pile of grilled peppers and onions.

1. Prepare a charcoal grill for two-zone cooking and build a medium-high fire, or heat a gas grill to high. Carefully wipe the preheated grates with a lightly oiled paper towel. Using a grill brush, scrape the grill grates clean, then carefully wipe with a lightly oiled towel again.

2. Grill the squash and corn over direct heat, turning as needed for even cooking, until lightly charred on all sides, 5 to 6 minutes. Set aside to cool.

3. Brush the panela slices with olive oil and grill until charred and browned, 1 to 2 minutes per side. Dice the grilled squash and transfer to a bowl. Trim the corn kernels from cob and add to the squash, along with the cilantro, oregano, lime juice, and a drizzle of olive oil. Stir to combine and season with salt and more lime juice as desired.

4. Grill the tortillas over direct heat until lightly charred, about 30 seconds per side. Keep warm in a basket or wrapped in a kitchen towel.

5. Spread a layer of the salsa on the bottom of a shallow dish or plate. Nestle slices of grilled panela in the salsa. Serve immediately with the squash-corn mixture and charred tortillas on the side.

State Park Potatoes (aka how to prepare a swoon-worthy gratin in the woods)

Serves 4

2 pounds (900g) Yukon gold potatoes, unpeeled and sliced ¼ inch (6mm) thick

2 shallots, thinly sliced

½ cup (120ml) olive oil

2 teaspoons freshly chopped thyme leaves

Kosher salt and freshly ground black pepper

4 ounces (115g) fresh goat cheese

4 to 8 thin slices speck (optional)

Is there a better package to open than one containing tender potatoes, fragrant browned shallots, and creamy goat cheese? Not in my book. We've made these potato and cheese packets at home as a satisfying main course and on camping trips to serve with steak. Speck (smoked cured pork) isn't essential, but it adds incredible flavor and bastes the potatoes as they cook.

1. Prepare a charcoal grill for two-zone cooking and build a medium fire, or heat a gas grill to medium-high. Carefully wipe the preheated grates with a lightly oiled paper towel. Using a grill brush, scrape the grill grates clean, then carefully wipe with a lightly oiled towel again.

2. In a large bowl, generously season the potatoes, shallots, olive oil, and thyme with salt and pepper and toss to combine. Cut 4 sheets of heavy-duty aluminum foil into 14 by 8–inch (36 by 20cm) rectangles. Place each rectangle shiny side down. Scoop one-quarter of the potato mixture in the middle. Top with a quarter of the goat cheese and speck. Fold the top half of the foil over the potatoes and bring the top and bottom edges together. Fold the edges over several times to make a tight seal. Prepare the remaining packages the same way.

3. When you're ready to cook, place the foil packages on the grate over indirect heat. Close the grill (venting appropriately for indirect cooking) and cook, rotating every now and then for even cooking, until the packets are puffed and the potatoes are tender, 30 to 40 minutes. To test for doneness, open 1 small corner of a packet (using caution as escaping steam will be very hot) and use a paring knife to pierce (and/or taste) a portion of a slice. Serve warm.

Grilling in Advance

Aluminum foil packets of potatoes (and other vegetables) hold beautifully: Once they're done, you can keep packets warm in a cooler heat zone while you cook something else (say a steak). (Or if your grill has an upper-tier rack, place the packets there.) Other dishes that hold well in these cooler zones—think about them like your low oven—include chicken thighs, corn on the cob, grilled onions and peppers, and grilled pita, naan, or other breads. If you need to hold the breads for more than 15 minutes, just wrap them in foil so they don't dry out.

Grilled Cheese & Mushrooms

Makes 2 sandwiches

8 ounces (225g) wild mushrooms (such as shiitake, oyster, hen-of-the-woods, or matsutake), stemmed

8 ounces (225g) cremini mushrooms, stemmed

Olive oil, for drizzling

Kosher salt and freshly ground black pepper

½ cup (110g) unsalted butter

2 teaspoons fish sauce (preferably Red Boat)

Two ½-inch-thick (1.3cm) slices of miche or another artisan bread, cut from the widest part of the round

4 ounces (115g) Gorgonzola dolce, other blue cheese, or raclette

The trick to maximizing the savory flavor of grilled mushrooms is basting them with butter—spiked with fish sauce—as they cook. To find the right cheese for the revved-up umami, John Antonelli, owner of Antonelli's Cheese Shop in Austin, encouraged me to embrace "fungus with fungus" via Gorgonzola dolce or Smokey Blue from Rogue Creamery in Oregon (it's smoked over hazelnut shells). The result is a decidedly grown-up grilled cheese. If you prefer pure gooey goodness, use raclette—its savory note is a natural ally for the mushrooms. Or to ramp up the funky flavor even more, toss the grilled mushrooms with a pinch of bonito flakes. If you want to temper the deep, earthy flavors in this sandwich, add a couple of thin slices of ripe tomato, Pickled Banana Peppers (page 180), or arugula.

While you should never use your spatula to "press" burgers, steaks, or other meats while they grill (you'll be pressing out their delicious juices and end up with a dry piece of meat), pressing—not mashing but melding—this sandwich as you would for a *pan bagnat* after grilling is an important step that fuses flavors for a more satisfying experience. A hearty-crusted bread like miche or ciabatta can easily hold up to the weight of a skillet.

1. In a bowl, drizzle the mushrooms with enough olive oil to lightly coat, season with salt and pepper, and toss to combine.

2. Prepare a charcoal grill for two-zone cooking and build a medium fire, or heat a gas grill to medium-high. Carefully wipe the preheated grates with a lightly oiled paper towel. Using a grill brush, scrape the grill grates clean, then carefully wipe with a lightly oiled towel again. If you're using a grill basket, allow it to heat for 10 minutes before cooking.

3. Melt the butter in a small cast-iron skillet on the grill over direct heat, then stir in the fish sauce. Move to a cooler zone to keep warm.

4. Grill the mushrooms, gill side up, over direct heat for 20 to 25 minutes, basting every now and then with the fish sauce butter and turning as needed for even cooking. If using a grill basket, move the basket off the heat as necessary to avoid flare-ups and, depending on your fire, rotate the basket 1 quarter turn every 5 minutes for even cooking. Remove from the heat.

CONTINUED

5. Cut each slice of bread in half crosswise. Slice the mushrooms as desired for easy eating (I leave shiitakes whole) and slice the cheese to fit the bread. Brush 1 side of each bread slice with the fish sauce butter. Divide mushrooms and cheese between 2 of the slices and then top with another slice, butter side up. Use a long-handled spatula to press the sandwich together. Grill until the bread is charred and the cheese has melted, 2 to 3 minutes per side. Transfer sandwiches to a baking sheet lined with parchment paper, cover with aluminum foil, and weight them down with a cast-iron skillet. Allow the sandwiches to meld for about 5 minutes, and then slice into desired size.

Why Bother Preheating a Grill Basket?

Preheating a grill basket is just like preheating a cast-iron skillet before cooking. When the metal basket is hot, foods are less likely to stick, and because the ingredients are lightly coated in olive oil, they benefit from that initial sizzle of a sear the minute they hit the grill.

Broccoli Spears with Crispy Cheese Crust

Serves 2 to 4

2 heads broccoli

Olive oil, for drizzling

Kosher salt and freshly
ground black pepper

½ teaspoon red pepper
flakes or chopped dried
arbol chile (stemmed and
seeded), plus more as
desired for heat

1½ cups (150g) coarsely
grated Parmesan, Asiago,
aged cheddar, or Gouda

Lemon wedges

Like roasting, a grill enhances the vegetable's natural sweetness and creates salty, crunchy browned bits that add an entirely different layer of appeal. When charred by the heat of a grill, brassicas like broccoli—particularly big, meaty stalks—offer a satisfying range of flavors and textures that warrant top billing. I prefer to grill large spears of broccoli because they're easier to wrangle and fun to eat with a knife and fork, but you can use broccolini or large florets of Romanesco broccoli instead. After they're branded with an initial char, the spears are transferred to a cast-iron skillet, covered with a blanket of grated Parmesan (or another aged cheese) and finished in a closed grill. The ambient heat melts the cheese and creates a crispy crust reminiscent of *frico*, lacy Parmesan crackers. Salsa Verde (page 176), Pickled Mustard Seeds (page 176), or Sumac Yogurt Sauce (page 176) would be delicious additions to the plate.

1. Prepare a charcoal grill for two-zone cooking and build a medium-high fire, or heat a gas grill to high. Carefully wipe the preheated grates with a lightly oiled paper towel. Using a grill brush, scrape the grill grates clean, then carefully wipe with a lightly oiled towel again. Preheat a cast-iron skillet for 10 minutes before cooking.

2. While the grill heats, use a paring knife to trim the bottom inch or two from the stems and peel the stems. Slice the broccoli heads into long spears (the florets should be attached to a long portion of stem). Place any florets that break loose in a mixing bowl. Drizzle the spears with olive oil and season with salt, black pepper, and chile.

3. Grill the broccoli over direct heat until evenly charred, 4 to 6 minutes per side, moving to indirect heat as needed to prevent the stalks from burning. Grill any small broccoli florets that break loose in the preheated cast-iron skillet, tossing often, until browned and crispy, 3 to 4 minutes.

4. Add the spears to the cast-iron skillet and place on the grill grate over direct heat. Sprinkle with the cheese, close the grill, and cook until the cheese is melted and the broccoli is crisp-tender, 4 to 5 minutes. Serve warm or at room temperature with lemon wedges.

Provoleta with Dandelion & Toasted Almonds

Serves 2 to 4

1 shallot, thinly sliced

2 tablespoons sherry vinegar

8 ounces (225g) aged provolone (round, half-round, or wedge) or another semihard cheese (such as asadero or Asiago)

¼ cup (60ml) plus 2 tablespoons olive oil, plus more for drizzling

2 tablespoons freshly chopped oregano

1 teaspoon red pepper flakes

2 tablespoons blood orange juice or regular orange juice

1 tablespoon Dijon mustard

Kosher salt and freshly ground black pepper

1 bunch dandelion greens (or watercress or arugula), stems and any thick ribs trimmed

⅓ cup (45g) coarsely chopped toasted almonds or hazelnuts

Grilled bread (see page 21)

In Argentina, grilled provolone cheese—or *provoleta*—is a tease, typically eaten on bread before an *asado*, a belt-busting marathon of grilled meats. But when served with bitter greens (a nice way to balance richness), a bright citrus vinaigrette, and crunchy toasted nuts, grilled provolone becomes a decadent "salad" that delivers a heavy dose of comfort. Argentine provolone is typically served in rounds, but it's difficult to source here. You'll get great results with aged provolone from Wisconsin or another semihard cheese like asadero or Asiago (typically sold in wedges or half-rounds). Unlike baked feta, aged provolone doesn't become custardy when cooked; it takes on a fantastic chewy, yielding texture that's fun to slather on grilled bread.

1. Prepare a charcoal grill for two-zone cooking and build a medium-high fire, or heat a gas grill to high. Carefully wipe the preheated grates with a lightly oiled paper towel. Using a grill brush, scrape the grill grates clean, then carefully wipe with a lightly oiled towel again.

2. Combine the shallot and vinegar in a bowl. In another bowl, drizzle the cheese with olive oil and sprinkle with the oregano and red pepper flakes. Use your hands to rub the seasonings evenly over the cheese.

3. Whisk the orange juice and Dijon into the shallots. Whisk in the olive oil and season with salt and pepper.

4. Grill the cheese over direct heat until grill marks appear and the cheese begins to soften, about 2 minutes. Use a metal spatula and a decisive push to lift the cheese and flip it over; if it sticks, use a two-pronged fork to help scrape the tasty browned bits from the grates. Grill until grill marks appear on the second side, another 1 to 2 minutes. Use the spatula and two-pronged fork to transfer the cheese to a serving dish or, if you want to keep it warm until serving, a small cast-iron skillet placed on the cooler portion of the grill.

5. When you're ready to serve, toss the greens with the vinaigrette and place them on a serving platter; top with the warm cheese and the toasted nuts (alternatively, you can divide the greens and cheese into individual servings). Serve immediately, with grilled bread on the side.

Charred Greens &
Smoky Salads

Grilled Escarole & Sweet Peppers with Pecorino Dressing

Serves 4

½ cup (120ml) olive oil, plus more for coating

2 cloves garlic, thinly sliced

2 tablespoons fresh lemon juice

2 tablespoons red wine vinegar

2 teaspoons Dijon mustard

¼ to ½ cup (25 to 50g) grated Pecorino, plus more for serving

Kosher salt and freshly ground black pepper

2 heads escarole, rinsed and dried

8 ounces (225g) sweet mini peppers

Like its creator, my friend Susan Spicer, the chef of Bayona, Mondo, and Rosedale in New Orleans, this salad has plenty of personality. The heat of a grill (along with a creamy toasted garlic dressing) tempers the peppery bite of escarole and other bitter greens. Lightly charred sweet peppers add a burst of color and sweetness that balances the assertive flavors. The cool thing about grilling escarole and other sturdy chicories is that they wilt but still retain a satisfying texture. The result is a hearty knife-and-fork salad that makes a simple but surprising meal on its own, or a delicious sidekick to grilled lamb chops or eggplant. Serve leftovers the next day cold, as a smoky riff on *horta* (the Greek salad of boiled bitter greens).

1. Prepare a charcoal grill for two-zone cooking and build a medium-high fire, or heat a gas grill to high. Carefully wipe the preheated grates with a lightly oiled paper towel. Using a grill brush, scrape the grill grates clean, then carefully wipe with a lightly oiled towel again. If you're using a grill basket, allow it to preheat 10 minutes before cooking.

2. On the stove top, heat ½ cup (120ml) of the olive oil and the garlic in a small skillet over medium-low heat until the garlic is lightly tanned and starting to crisp, and then remove the skillet from the heat. Combine the lemon juice, vinegar, and Dijon in a blender and process for about 30 seconds, then slowly add the infused oil and garlic and process until silky and emulsified. Pour the dressing into a bowl, whisk in ¼ cup (25g) of Pecorino, and season with salt and black pepper. The dressing should start to thicken and be creamy and pleasantly tart-salty; if it's too thin or tart, add additional oil and cheese as desired.

3. Trim the escarole as needed, removing tired leaves. Quarter the escarole heads lengthwise, keeping the stem intact to help the leaves hold together on the grill. Place in a large bowl, drizzle with enough olive oil to lightly coat, season with salt and black pepper, and use your hands to gently combine.

4. Grill the escarole over direct heat until lightly charred, 30 to 45 seconds on each side; set aside. Toss the peppers in the same bowl (adding additional oil, if necessary, to lightly coat them), season with salt and black pepper, and grill over direct heat until lightly charred, about 2 minutes on each side. Arrange the escarole and peppers on a large platter, drizzle with dressing, and top with additional Pecorino.

Chicories with Charred Scallion Dressing, Crispy Egg & Nori Bread Crumbs

Serves 2

Charred Scallion Dressing

1 cup (240ml) Greek yogurt

Finely grated zest and juice of 1 lemon

2 tablespoons olive oil, plus more as needed

1 tablespoon Dijon mustard

1 tablespoon honey

1 clove garlic, finely grated

2 tablespoons freshly chopped dill

Kosher salt and freshly ground black pepper

1 bunch scallions, trimmed

2 slices day-old bread

¼ cup (5g) crumbled nori

2 tablespoons sesame seeds (black or white)

1 teaspoon gochugaru (Korean red pepper), plus more as desired

6 to 8 ounces (170 to 225g) mixed chicories (such as Treviso, radicchio, frisée, and endive)

2 large eggs

Flaky salt

4 chives, cut into ½-inch (1.3cm) lengths

Lenoir, our friends Todd Duplechan and Jessica Maher's restaurant in South Austin, is devoted to "hot-weather food": spicy, citrusy, and acidic preparations that suit the weather in Texas and other steamy zones around the world. Todd's version of this salad is more complicated, but I followed his lead to combine grilled chicories with a charred scallion dressing, crispy egg, and furikake-inspired bread crumbs (a riff on the Japanese seasoning made with dried fish, sesame seeds, and seaweed). When they're in season, feel free to use Meyer lemons in the dressing; their sweetness plays well with the bitter greens—just be sure to adjust ingredients as necessary to compensate for their lower acidity.

1. Prepare a charcoal grill for two-zone cooking and build a medium fire, or heat a gas grill to medium-high. Carefully wipe the preheated grates with a lightly oiled paper towel. Using a grill brush, scrape the grill grates clean, then carefully wipe with a lightly oiled towel again.

2. To make the dressing, in a bowl, whisk together the yogurt, lemon zest and juice, olive oil, Dijon, honey, and garlic. Whisk in the dill and season with kosher salt and pepper. Thin the dressing with olive oil as needed for consistency.

3. Grill the bread over direct heat until grill marks appear on both sides, about a minute per side. Let cool, then crumble the bread slices into the bowl of a food processor. Add the nori, sesame seeds, gochugaru, and a pinch of kosher salt and pulse into coarse crumbs.

4. Trim the chicories as needed, removing tired leaves. Halve or quarter the chicory heads lengthwise, keeping the stem intact to help the leaves hold together on the grill. Place the chicories and scallions in a bowl, drizzle with enough olive oil to lightly coat, season with salt and pepper, and gently toss to combine. Grill over direct heat until lightly charred, 2 to 3 minutes per side.

5. Divide the chicories between 2 plates. Chop the charred scallions and stir them into the yogurt dressing. On the stove top, fry the eggs in olive oil over medium-high heat until the edges are browned and the yolk is partially set (do not flip); season with black pepper and flaky salt. Drizzle the chicories with the dressing, top with an egg, and sprinkle with flaky salt, the bread crumbs, and the chives.

The Cabbage Patch Wedge

Serves 4

2 small green cabbages

½ cup plus 2 tablespoons (150ml) extra-virgin olive oil, plus more for drizzling

Kosher salt and freshly ground black pepper

¼ cup (60ml) cider vinegar or champagne vinegar

1 tablespoon Dijon mustard

1 tablespoon honey

½ cup (70g) crumbled blue cheese (such as Roquefort)

1 cup (150g) yellow or orange cherry tomatoes (preferably Sweet 100s or another small variety), halved

5 to 6 ounces (140 to 170g) cooked smoked bacon, crumbled

6 to 8 radishes (any variety), thinly sliced

¼ cup (10g) chives, cut into ½-inch (1.3cm) lengths

Brassicas like brussels sprouts, broccoli, and cabbage benefit from a high-heat char that transforms their rubbery, raw texture into something tender and toothsome, with a whiff of smoky sweetness. To maintain some crunch at the core, you'll want to use a two-part cooking process: high heat for charring, followed by lower, indirect heat that allows the sturdy wedges to mostly cook through. The nutty sweetness and hardy structure of grilled cabbage pair perfectly with a wedge salad's classic accompaniments: a crumbled blue cheese dressing, sweet cherry tomatoes, crumbled bacon, and chives.

1. Cut each cabbage lengthwise into 4 fat wedges, keeping the core intact to help it hold together on the grill. In a large bowl, drizzle the cabbages with enough olive oil to lightly coat, generously season with salt and pepper, and gently toss to combine.

2. Prepare a charcoal grill for two-zone cooking and build a medium-high fire, or heat a gas grill to high. Carefully wipe the preheated grates with a lightly oiled paper towel. Using a grill brush, scrape the grill grates clean, then carefully wipe with a lightly oiled towel again.

3. Grill the cabbage wedges over direct heat until charred on all sides, 4 to 6 minutes total. Transfer them to a cooler portion of the grill and cook until the interior has softened but still has a bit of crunch, 5 to 6 additional minutes. Use a paring knife or your fingers to test doneness. When the cabbages are cooked, transfer the wedges to a serving platter and let them cool briefly while you make the dressing.

4. In a bowl, whisk together the vinegar, Dijon, honey, ½ teaspoon salt, and plenty of pepper. Whisk in the ½ cup plus 2 tablespoons (150ml) olive oil until the mixture has emulsified. Stir in the blue cheese.

5. Drizzle the blue cheese dressing over the cabbage wedges and top with the cherry tomatoes, bacon, radishes, and chives.

Radicchio & Pears with Anchovy Bread Crumbs and Burrata

Serves 2 to 4

2 heads radicchio

2 pears (such as Bosc, Anjou, or any green speckled variety)

Olive oil, for drizzling

Kosher salt and freshly ground black pepper

2 slices day-old bread, plus more for sopping up oil and cheese

2 marinated anchovies, coarsely chopped

2 teaspoons fresh thyme leaves

About 2 tablespoons white wine vinegar

6 ounces (170g) fresh burrata, drained and patted dry

Fresh radicchio is bright and bitter, but grilled radicchio is multilayered and complex. Just a few minutes on the grill give the lovely white-veined magenta chicory deep caramelized notes—a transformation that shifts it from a first-course salad to a full-on meal. Adding fruit and a luscious fresh cheese creates a delicious balance of bitter, sweet, creamy, and crunchy. You don't want super-juicy pears here—they'll break down on the grill—but flavor-wise, you don't want them to be rock-hard either. Go with a firmer, fragrant variety that yields with some resistance to a sharp knife. I love to use mottled green heirloom pears that look like they were plucked from a Renaissance painting, but Red Bartlett, Bosc, or Concorde also work. You can stem and core the pears before grilling, but I prefer to leave them intact because it looks nicer and they hold up better on the grill. During the summer, swap out pears for peaches.

1. Prepare a charcoal grill for two-zone cooking and build a medium fire, or heat a gas grill to medium-high. Carefully wipe the preheated grates with a lightly oiled paper towel. Using a grill brush, scrape the grill grates clean, then carefully wipe with a lightly oiled towel again. If you're using a grill basket, allow it to heat for 10 minutes before cooking.

2. Quarter the radicchio heads lengthwise, keeping the stem intact to help the leaves hold together on the grill, and quarter the pears lengthwise. Place the radicchio and pears in a large bowl, drizzle with enough olive oil to lightly coat, season generously with salt and pepper, and toss with your hands to evenly coat.

3. Grill the bread over direct heat until grill marks appear on both sides, about a minute per side. Let cool, then crumble the bread into a food processor. Add the anchovies, thyme, a pinch each of salt and pepper, and pulse into coarse crumbs.

4. Grill the pears over direct heat until grill marks appear on both cut sides, 2 to 3 minutes per side. Remove, then grill the radicchio until lightly charred on all sides, 4 to 5 minutes total. In a large bowl, gently toss the radicchio and pears with additional olive oil and the vinegar to coat lightly.

5. Arrange the radicchio and pears on a platter or divide among plates. Top with the bread crumbs and generous spoonfuls of burrata. Grind pepper over the top and serve.

Asparagus & String Beans with Smoky Romesco

Serves 4

2 bunches asparagus
(about 2 pounds/900g)

1 pound (450g) green,
purple, or yellow wax
beans (preferably a
combination)

1 thick slice country-style
bread

2 large red bell peppers—
halved, cored, and seeded

2 Fresno chiles

½ red onion, cut into
thick wedges

⅓ cup (80ml) extra-virgin
olive oil, plus more for
drizzling

2 plum tomatoes, halved

¼ cup (35g) skinned
roasted hazelnuts or
almonds

1 tablespoon sherry vinegar,
plus more as desired

2 teaspoons freshly
chopped thyme or
marjoram leaves

1 teaspoon smoked paprika

1 clove garlic or 1 teaspoon
Smoked Garlic (page 86)

Kosher salt and freshly
ground black pepper

The game plan here is firing a pretty mix of long, thin vegetables that cook in a flash to serve with a Spanish-style romesco— a red pepper sauce enriched with nuts and grilled bread. Feel free to change up the mix with young carrots, baby pattypan squash, sugar snap peas, or Chinese long beans, adjusting cooking times as needed. If you're lucky enough to have leftovers, chop the grilled vegetables and scramble them with eggs and a few spoonfuls of the smoky sauce.

1. Prepare a charcoal grill for two-zone cooking and build a medium fire, or heat a gas grill to medium-high. Carefully wipe the preheated grates with a lightly oiled paper towel. Using a grill brush, scrape the grill grates clean, then carefully wipe with a lightly oiled towel again. If you're using a grill basket, allow it to heat for 10 minutes before cooking.

2. Snap fibrous ends from the asparagus (or if the asparagus is fat, peel the ends). Trim the stem ends from the wax beans.

3. Grill the bread over direct heat until grill marks appear on both sides, about a minute per side.

4. In a bowl, toss the bell peppers, Fresno chiles, and onion with enough olive oil to lightly coat. Place the vegetables perpendicular to the grates (or in a preheated grill basket) and grill over direct heat, turning and rotating as needed for even cooking, until lightly charred on all sides, about 5 minutes for the peppers and chiles and 6 to 7 minutes for the onion. Set aside the onion. Transfer the charred bell peppers and chiles to a bowl and cover with a kitchen towel (this will make their skins easier to remove). Grill the tomatoes over direct heat until charred on both sides, 2 to 3 minutes per side. When they're cool enough to handle, remove most of their skins and seeds. Gently remove the skins of the bell peppers. Stem the Fresno chiles.

5. Process the bell peppers, chiles, onion, and tomatoes along with the nuts, vinegar, thyme, smoked paprika, garlic, and 1 teaspoon salt into a coarse puree. Cube the grilled bread, add to the mixture, and process until combined. Drizzle in the ⅓ cup (80ml) olive oil and process to make a thick puree. Taste for seasoning and add more salt and black pepper as desired.

6. Reheat the grill basket for 10 minutes before cooking, if using, and then grill the asparagus and wax beans until golden brown and lightly charred, about 6 minutes. Serve warm or at room temperature with romesco.

Rustic Winter Squash with Arugula & Apples

Serves 4

1 bunch scallions

1 butternut squash

1 acorn squash

A few handfuls arugula (preferably not baby)

1 Honeycrisp apple, cored and thinly sliced

¼ cup (5g) fresh mint leaves

3 tablespoons toasted pumpkin seeds (pepitas)

1 to 2 tablespoons cider vinegar

Extra-virgin olive oil, for drizzling

Flaky salt

Freshly ground black pepper

All too often, winter squash preparations fall to the heavy side and are too sweet for my tastes. But this vibrant combination, inspired by Joshua McFadden, chef at Ava Gene's in Portland, is a beauty—a variety of winter squashes are grilled almost to the point of looking burnt, which creates tremendous complexity as the heat caramelizes their sugars. Another cool trick: Only one side is grilled, so each piece offers a mix of deep caramelization and the bright flavor of squash that's just cooked through. Feel free to use whichever squash you love. A tumble of peppery arugula, mint, and a crisp apple keeps this salad feeling snappy.

1. Prepare a charcoal grill for two-zone cooking and build a medium-high fire, or heat a gas grill to high. Carefully wipe the preheated grates with a lightly oiled paper towel. Using a grill brush, scrape the grill grates clean, then carefully wipe with a lightly oiled towel again.

2. While the grill heats, trim the scallions and slice them on the bias. Soak in ice water until very crisp, about 30 minutes, and then drain and dry on paper towels.

3. Halve the butternut squash lengthwise, quarter the acorn squash vertically, and scrape out the seeds (a grapefruit spoon works well for this).

4. Working in batches if necessary, grill the squashes over direct heat, skin side down, until deeply charred, 6 to 8 minutes. Set aside to cool slightly. When cool enough to handle, use your hands to peel most (or all) of the skin. Cut into bite-size pieces.

5. In a large bowl, combine the squashes, scallions, arugula, apple, mint, and pumpkin seeds. Drizzle with the vinegar and enough olive oil to coat, generously season with flaky salt and pepper, and toss to combine. Taste, adjust as desired (adding more salt or vinegar, if needed), and serve immediately.

Grilled Vegetable Salad with Brown Butter Vinaigrette

Serves 6

Brown Butter Vinaigrette

½ cup (110g) unsalted butter

¼ cup (60ml) sherry vinegar

2 tablespoons minced shallot

2 tablespoons minced garlic

1 tablespoon Dijon mustard

½ cup (120ml) extra-virgin olive oil

Kosher salt and freshly ground black pepper

1 head cauliflower, sliced into large florets

18 baby carrots, cut on the bias into bite-size pieces

10 large radishes, trimmed

Olive oil, for drizzling

Kosher salt and freshly ground black pepper

6 ounces (170g) arugula

Leaves from 6 sprigs mint, torn

12 ounces (340g) fresh goat cheese, crumbled

Whenever I spy colorful heads of cauliflower (yellow, purple, snowy white) or romanesco at the market, I yearn to make this salad from *Collards & Carbonara*, the excellent cookbook by Michael Hudman and Anthony Ticer, chefs at Hog & Hominy in Memphis. Their notion of grilling hearty winter vegetables and dressing them with a rich dressing was somewhat of a revelation. For the most striking result, use as many colors and varieties of vegetables as possible. They call for baby carrots, but I always use freshly harvested local carrots (orange, purple, and gold when possible) because the "fresh from the garden" flavor is so much better.

1. Prepare a charcoal grill for two-zone cooking and build a medium-high fire, or heat a gas grill to high. Carefully wipe the preheated grates with a lightly oiled paper towel. Using a grill brush, scrape the grill grates clean, then carefully wipe with a lightly oiled towel again. If you're using a grill basket, allow it to heat for 10 minutes before cooking.

2. To make the vinaigrette, on the stove top or grill, melt the butter in a saucepan over medium heat, then turn the heat to medium-low and simmer gently, swirling the pan often, until the butter is browned and smells nutty, about 10 minutes. Let cool to room temperature. In a large bowl, whisk together the brown butter, vinegar, shallot, garlic, and Dijon. Whisk in the oil and season to taste with salt and pepper. (You can also puree it in a blender if you prefer.)

3. In a large bowl, toss the cauliflower, carrots, and radishes with enough olive oil to lightly coat. Season generously with salt and pepper.

4. Grill the vegetables over direct heat and cook, turning once, until pronounced grill marks form, about 2 minutes per side. You want to have nice caramelization on the vegetables, but they should still have some integrity.

5. Put the vegetables in a large bowl and let cool slightly. Add the arugula, mint, and vinaigrette, and toss well. Divide the vegetables evenly among 6 salad plates. Top with the goat cheese and serve.

Smoky Fattoush with Buttermilk Dressing

Serves 2 to 4

½ cup (120ml) well-shaken buttermilk

½ cup (120ml) extra-virgin olive oil, plus more for drizzling

2 tablespoons white balsamic vinegar

2 tablespoons fresh lemon juice

Kosher salt and freshly ground black pepper

3 heads baby romaine

4 Persian cucumbers

2 cups (270g) cherry tomatoes (preferably small Sweet 100s or an oval variety)

4 scallions, thinly sliced on the bias

4 to 6 radishes (any variety), thinly sliced

½ cup (25g) coarsely chopped Italian parsley

½ cup (20g) coarsely chopped fresh cilantro (leaves and tender stems)

2 pita breads (preferably day-old)

1 cup (150g) crumbled feta cheese

Back in the day, late-night cabs from my cubicle in Manhattan to my apartment in Brooklyn Heights often meant take-out fattoush, the Middle Eastern chopped salad made with crunchy bits of pita bread. These days, when I make it at home, I like to grill the greens—usually spears of romaine lettuce or dandelion—to add a smoky depth that makes the salad complex and satisfying. Then I geek out over the prettiest vegetables I can find: sweet Persian cucumbers, radishes, cherry tomatoes, and plenty of fresh herbs. Sliced grilled chicken breast (see page 146) would be great on top, too.

1. Prepare a charcoal grill for two-zone cooking and build a medium-high fire, or heat a gas grill to high. Carefully wipe the preheated grates with a lightly oiled paper towel. Using a grill brush, scrape the grill grates clean, then carefully wipe with a lightly oiled towel again. If you're using a grill basket, allow it to heat for 10 minutes before cooking.

2. In a medium bowl, whisk together the buttermilk, olive oil, 1 tablespoon of the vinegar, and the lemon juice. Season with salt and pepper.

3. Quarter the romaine heads lengthwise, keeping the stem intact to help the leaves hold together on the grill. In a large bowl, drizzle the romaine with enough olive oil to lightly coat, season with salt, and use your hands to gently toss until evenly coated.

4. Peel lengthwise stripes into the cucumber by leaving some skin on, trim the ends, halve them lengthwise, and thinly slice them on the bias. Place the cucumbers, cherry tomatoes, scallions, radishes, parsley, and cilantro in a bowl. Add the remaining tablespoon of vinegar and a pinch of salt and gently toss to combine. Set aside to marinate.

5. Grill the pita bread over direct heat until charred on both sides, a minute per side. While the bread is still warm and pliable, slice it into 1½-inch (4cm) squares (otherwise, let the bread cool until crisp and then break it up with your hands). Grill the lettuce quarters over direct heat until lightly charred on all sides, 3 to 4 minutes, and then place them on a platter to cool slightly. Give the buttermilk dressing another whisk and pour half of it over the marinated vegetables; add half of the pita and toss to combine. Pour the remaining dressing over the grilled romaine, top with marinated vegetables, feta, remaining pita, and a grind of pepper. Serve immediately.

Grilled & Coal-Roasted
Vegetable Mains

Artichokes with Grilled Lemon Mayo & Fresh Herbs

Serves 4

4 large artichokes

1 large lemon

Grilled Lemon Mayo

2 large lemons, halved

⅓ cup (80ml) extra-virgin olive oil

3 tablespoons freshly chopped herbs (any combination of oregano, marjoram, or parsley)

1 teaspoon freshly minced lemon thyme leaves

1 teaspoon minced Smoked Garlic (page 86) or regular garlic

Kosher salt and freshly ground black pepper

3 tablespoons mayonnaise (preferably Duke's)

Grilled bread (see page 21)

Maybe it's their otherworldly beauty (have you seen the spectacular purple flowers in bloom?), their ancient pedigree (artichokes were beloved by ancient Greeks and Romans), or simply that they require a bit of effort to enjoy, but for me, artichokes transform any meal into a luxurious occasion. They're at their best—and easiest to prepare—when cooked quickly over a hot fire, particularly when served with luscious lemon mayo made with the smoky juices and pulp of grilled lemon. You can serve the creamy dressing on the side for dipping, but I prefer to toss it with the artichokes so it seeps into every crack and crevice. For a heartier meal, grill young carrots, spears of summer squash, or merguez sausages alongside the artichokes.

1. Prepare a charcoal grill for two-zone cooking and build a medium fire, or heat a gas grill to medium-high. Carefully wipe the preheated grates with a lightly oiled paper towel. Using a grill brush, scrape the grill grates clean, then carefully wipe with a lightly oiled towel again.

2. On the stove top, bring a large pot of salted water to a boil. Trim the stem of each artichoke to 1 inch (2.5cm) long, then snap off the dark outer leaves. Use a sharp knife to trim off the top 1 inch (2.5cm) of the artichoke leaves. Use a paring knife to peel the dark green skin from the stem and base of artichoke. Slice each artichoke in half lengthwise. Use a paring knife to remove the choke and the purple, prickly-tipped leaves from the center of each half. Place the prepped artichokes in a large bowl of cold water with the juice of a lemon. Continue with the remaining artichokes.

3. Drain the artichokes, then cook in the boiling water until just tender when pierced with a sharp knife, about 12 minutes. Drain the artichokes.

4. Grill artichokes cut side down over direct heat, turning occasionally, until tender and lightly charred in spots, about 10 minutes. Nestle the remaining 2 lemons, cut side down, among the artichokes and cook until they're charred and softened, about 4 minutes.

5. To make the mayo, squeeze the juice from the warm grilled lemons into a bowl, discarding the seeds, and then scoop out the flesh, coarsely chop, and add to the juice. Whisk in the olive oil, herbs, and garlic. Season with salt and pepper to taste. Whisk in the mayo. Serve the warm artichokes with mayo and grilled bread.

Smoky Eggplant Dip with Grilled Pita

Serves 4 to 6

3 large or 4 medium eggplants (about 3 pounds/1.4kg)

2 small onions, unpeeled

1 tablespoon fresh thyme leaves

1 large clove garlic

Kosher salt and freshly ground black pepper

¼ cup (10g) freshly chopped parsley

2 heaping tablespoons tahini

2 teaspoons fresh lemon juice

2 tablespoons of your best extra-virgin olive oil, plus more for brushing

Pita bread

Cooking eggplant directly on a bed of glowing coals dusted with ash blisters and blackens their skin and turns their flesh tender and smoky (unfortunately, you can't achieve this on a gas grill). They'll collapse onto themselves but still hold their shape. The smoky flesh creates an incredible riff on baba ghanoush, the beloved Middle Eastern appetizer. Served alongside feta cheese, oil-cured olives, grilled pita, and perhaps some store-bought dolmades, this luscious spread can star in a light summer meal, and leftovers make a fantastic lunch. Use small onions because they'll become tender faster.

1. Prepare a charcoal grill for one-zone cooking and build a medium fire.

2. When the coals are covered with ash and glowing orangish red with no black remaining (about 35 minutes after you light the coals), place the eggplants and onions directly on the coals and cook, using tongs to turn them occasionally, until skins are blackened and tender and the eggplants have collapsed, 10 to 15 minutes for the eggplants, 20 to 25 minutes for the onions.

3. Let the eggplants and onions cool slightly on a rimmed baking sheet. Cut the eggplant open lengthwise and use a spoon to scrape out the tender insides; discard the charred skin and stem. Place the eggplant flesh in a colander and let excess moisture drain for 15 to 30 minutes (as time allows).

4. Meanwhile, peel, quarter, and dice the onion. Place the onion, thyme, garlic, and ½ teaspoon salt in a food processor and pulse into a coarse puree. Add the drained eggplant flesh, parsley, tahini, lemon juice, and a few grindings of pepper and process until the mixture is combined but still has some texture. Taste and adjust seasonings as desired. Transfer to a serving bowl and drizzle with your best olive oil.

5. Before serving, brush pita bread with additional olive oil (this isn't necessary but creates a richer flavor), and grill until lightly charred, a minute or two per side. If your fire has gotten extremely low, you can also heat the pita bread directly on the glowing coals, using long-handled tongs to flip after a minute or two on each side. Lightly salt the pita bread, slice into wedges if desired, and serve warm alongside the dip.

Coal-Roasted Spaghetti Squash, Two Ways

Serves 4

2 spaghetti squash

Olive oil

Kosher salt and freshly ground black pepper

Aglio e Olio (page 86) or Charred Tomato Sauce (page 86)

Most of the recipes in this book can be prepared on either a gas or charcoal grill, but achieving the transformative effect of coal-roasted vegetables requires glowing embers—you just don't get the same flavor without a fire. When finishing spaghetti squash on the grill, the flesh won't visually change much, but the blackened underside imparts a deep smokiness that permeates every strand after it's tossed—even more so on the second day. While this recipe requires some advance roasting (the squash needs 30 to 40 minutes in the oven before it's placed on the coals), use that time to fire up the grill, prep a salad, and make one of the two delicious sauce options on page 86.

1. Heat the oven to 375°F (190°C).

2. Halve the squash lengthwise and scrape out the seeds (a grapefruit spoon works well). Lightly coat both sides of the squash with olive oil and generously season the flesh side with salt and pepper. Place the squash cut side down on a baking sheet and roast until the flesh is just tender, 30 to 40 minutes.

3. Meanwhile, prepare a charcoal grill for one-zone cooking and build a medium fire.

4. If you're serving with Charred Tomato Sauce, grill the tomatoes before the squash hits the grill (see page 86). When the coals are covered with ash and glowing orangish red with no black remaining (about 35 minutes after you light the coals), place the squash halves directly on the coals, cut side up, and cook until the squash is heated all the way through, about 15 minutes. You'll know it's done when juices begin to surface and bubbles form on top. The tough outer skins will get very black and charred, but they should remain intact.

5. Use tongs and a spatula to remove the squash from the grill and cool slightly. (Now is a good time to finish making your sauce). At this point, you can use a fork to loosen the tender squash strands and transfer them to a serving bowl or place each half on a plate. Serve with Aglio e Olio or Charred Tomato Sauce.

My Go-To Grilled Larder

My year-round staples include sauces that take meals to the next level,
as well as a few other secret weapons that enhance—or serve up—dinner in a flash.

Aglio e Olio

Calling all garlic lovers: This aromatic riff on the traditional garlic and oil pasta dish from Naples is fantastic drizzled over Coal-Roasted Spaghetti Squash (page 85). Heat ½ cup (120ml) olive oil and 2 cloves thinly sliced garlic in a small saucepan over medium heat until the garlic sizzles, about 4 minutes. Remove from the heat, cool slightly, and then whisk in the grated zest and juice of 1 lemon.

If you're serving on squash, drizzle the garlic oil over the warm squash strands (or divide among 4 halves) and season generously with freshly ground black pepper; use 2 forks to toss to combine. Top with flaky salt, red pepper flakes, and a shower of grated Pecorino and chopped fresh parsley. Serve immediately with additional grated Pecorino. *Also good with linguine or spaghetti, and drizzled over Basic Grilled Fish (page 112).*

Charred Tomato Sauce

What's better than a can of fire-roasted tomatoes? Sweet, smoky fresh tomatoes that you char yourself over a hot fire. This sauce is so flavorful that you should consider doubling the recipe and freezing half (see serving inspirations below).

Halve 4 plum tomatoes and grill, cut side down, until charred on both sides, 4 to 5 minutes. Place 1 clove garlic (regular garlic or Smoked Garlic, see right) and a generous pinch of kosher salt in a food processor and pulse to chop. Add the warm tomatoes (this will help "cook" the garlic so it won't be too sharp) and pulse until combined. Add 3 tablespoons extra-virgin olive oil, 1 tablespoon sherry vinegar, 2 tablespoons chopped fresh oregano, and freshly ground black pepper to taste and process until combined but not completely smooth. Taste for seasoning and adjust as desired. Refrigerate until needed. Serve over the warm squash strands (or divide among 4 halves) and top with crumbled goat cheese and chopped fresh parsley. *Good with Coal-Roasted Spaghetti Squash (page 85), Grilled Eggplant Gratin (opposite), Italian sausage and rigatoni, grilled chicken breasts (see page 146), and as a base for baked eggs.*

Smoked Garlic

Smoked garlic is easy to prepare while you're tackling something else on the grill, and it's a seductive flavor bomb that adds a smoky sweetness to pasta sauce, vinaigrettes, or soups. Soak 1 cup (90g) wood chips (applewood or oak) in water for 30 minutes. Meanwhile, prepare a charcoal grill for whatever else you're cooking and build a medium fire, or heat a gas grill to medium-high. Trim the tops from 3 garlic heads (just enough to reveal the cloves), place the heads cut side up in an aluminum foil packet, and drizzle with enough olive oil to lightly coat. Drain the wood chips and scatter them over the hot coals. If using a gas grill, put them in a perforated foil packet or smoker box and place directly over the flames. Place the garlic packet directly on coals, or move it up to the cooking grate if the heat feels particularly intense (you want the temperature moderate enough that the garlic softens and caramelizes before it gets overly black). Cook until the garlic is tender, 30 to 40 minutes. Let cool slightly, then transfer the heads and oil to a sealable glass jar. Add more oil to cover the garlic heads halfway, seal the jar, and store in the fridge for up to 1 month. *Smoked Garlic can enhance Grilled Lemon Mayo (page 81) or your favorite store-bought mayonnaise for instant aioli, Smoky Ratatouille (page 96), Smoky Tomato & Red Lentil Soup (page 107), and your favorite chili.*

Grilled Eggplant Gratin

With its charred tomato sauce and gooey cheese, this satisfying gratin (one of my go-to comfort dishes) is like a smoky riff on eggplant Parmesan. I might actually prefer this version—because the eggplant isn't breaded, it softens into a luscious texture while still retaining its character. Slice 2 eggplants into ½-inch (1.3cm) rounds, season with kosher salt, and place in a colander to drain for 20 minutes. Meanwhile, prepare a charcoal grill for two-zone cooking and build a medium fire, or heat a gas grill to medium-high. Pat the eggplant rounds dry with a paper towel, place them on a rimmed baking sheet, brush both sides with olive oil, and grill over direct heat, turning and rotating as needed for even cooking, until slightly charred and tender, 6 to 7 minutes. Coat an 8 by 8-inch (20 by 20cm) baking dish with olive oil and arrange 3 rows of alternating rounds of grilled eggplant and fresh mozzarella slices (you'll need about 16 ounces/455g), allowing rows to lean at a slight angle to fit the pan. Pour about 2 cups (475ml) Charred Tomato Sauce (opposite) over the eggplant, top with ½ cup (50g) grated Parmesan and ½ cup (55g) grilled bread crumbs (see page 21), if desired, and bake at 400°F (200°C) until the sauce bubbles and the cheese melts, about 25 minutes. Serve warm, or allow the gratin to cool completely, double-wrap in plastic, and freeze for a future feast (unwrap and reheat at 350°F/175°C until hot and bubbly). *Good with an arugula salad or a colorful mix of crunchy, shaved vegetables tossed with your favorite vinaigrette.*

Spicy Fish Sauce Vinaigrette

Spicy and tart from chiles and fresh lime juice, this workhorse dressing punches up just about everything. Prepare a charcoal grill for two-zone cooking and build a medium fire, or heat a gas grill to medium-high. Grill 2 serrano chiles and 1 clove garlic in a grill basket or small cast-iron skillet over direct heat, turning as needed for even charring, until serranos are blistered on all sides and garlic skin is blackened and mostly tender, 3 to 4 minutes for the serranos, 5 to 7 minutes for the garlic. Stem chiles (do not seed), peel and mince garlic, and combine them in a bowl with ½ cup (120ml) fish sauce (preferably Red Boat), ¼ cup (60ml) water, 2 tablespoons rice vinegar, 2 tablespoons fresh lime juice, and ¼ cup (50g) sugar. Stir to dissolve the sugar. Store in a sealed container in the fridge for up to 2 weeks. *Good with Salt-Crusted Snapper (page 130), chicken thighs (see page 145; add rice noodles and fresh herbs, if desired), grilled pork chops (see page 165), and any grilled vegetables.*

Smoked Beets & Black Lentils

Serves 4 to 6

2 cups (180g) wood chips (preferably applewood or oak)

4 baseball-size beets

2 tablespoons fruit vinegar (such as fig, elderberry, or cider), plus more as needed

Olive oil, for drizzling

Kosher salt and freshly ground black pepper

2 cups (400g) cooked black beluga lentils

¼ cup (30g) toasted chopped pistachios or hazelnuts

⅓ cup (50g) crumbled feta or shaved ricotta salata cheese

Freshly chopped cilantro or parsley

Why waste a bed of glowing embers? Coal-roasting dense vegetables like winter squash, onions, or beets is a brilliant way to make the most of the fire that's left behind after you've grilled something else over charcoal. The vegetables don't need much attention (just try to remember to turn them every 15 minutes or so), and they'll be the unexpected star of a future meal. In this recipe, beets take on a whiff of smoke from a scattering of wood chips. Their smoky sweetness plays beautifully alongside black lentils, but they're also great with chewy grains (such as farro or barley) or over a pool of lemony Greek yogurt. Smoked beets have plenty of personality, and they're enhanced by a wide range of fruity acids, so pull out that bottle of pomegranate, fig, or elderberry vinegar you've been saving. Because smoked beets have so much flavor, dress the lentils simply—their earthy flavor balances the dish.

1. Soak the wood chips in water for 30 minutes.

2. Prepare a charcoal grill for one-zone cooking and build a medium-high fire.

3. When the coals are covered with ash and glowing orangish red with no black remaining (about 35 minutes after lighting the coals), drain the wood chips and scatter them onto the coals. Vent the grill for smoking.

4. Nestle the beets into the embers and cook, turning every 15 minutes or so, until they're just tender when pierced with a knife, 45 to 50 minutes total. Transfer the beets to a plate to cool. At this point, you can wrap the unpeeled beets in aluminum foil and refrigerate them for up to 5 days. Using your hands, peel the blackened skin from the beets; use a knife or paper towel to remove any remaining blackened bits but do not rinse.

5. Use a mandoline to slice the beets crosswise into thin rounds. In a bowl, toss the beets with the vinegar, a generous drizzle of olive oil, and salt and pepper to taste. Taste for seasoning and adjust as desired; you'll want to add enough vinegar to balance the smokiness of the beets. At this point, you can let the beets marinate in the fridge for up to 3 days.

6. Serve the beets at room temperature on a platter or individual serving plates alongside the black lentils. Top both with a drizzle of olive oil, additional salt and pepper, nuts, cheese, and herbs.

Grilled Corn Nachos

Serves 4

4 ears corn, shucked

1 bunch scallions

1 cup (150g) small cherry tomatoes (optional)

3 tablespoons freshly chopped cilantro

1 tablespoon fresh lime juice, plus more as desired

Kosher salt

One 11-ounce (312g) bag regular or blue corn tortilla chips

One 15½-ounce (439g) can black beans, drained and rinsed

3 cups (330g) shredded Monterey Jack cheese

1 cup (110g) shredded Cotija

Mexican crema or sour cream, for drizzling

Sliced pickled jalapeños and/or Pickled Banana Peppers (optional; page 180)

Saying yes to nachos for dinner feels like rule breaking in the best way (jalapeños count as a vegetable, right?). This decision usually translates to a small party, with Grilled Satsuma Margaritas (page 17) for grown-ups and Mexican Cokes for kids. This recipe's fresh and hearty combination of grilled sweet corn tossed with fresh lime juice and cilantro, black beans, and the sharp flavor of aged Cotija cheese is more satisfying than the standard chips-and-cheese variety. And by the time you've prepped the vegetables, you're ready to place the baking sheet directly on the grate to cook in a closed grill until the cheese has melted—no oven required! Serve with your favorite red or green salsa (mine's on page 151).

1. Prepare a charcoal grill for one-zone cooking and build a medium fire, or heat a gas grill to medium-high. Carefully wipe the preheated grates with a lightly oiled paper towel. Using a grill brush, scrape the grill grates clean, then carefully wipe with a lightly oiled towel again. Allow a grill basket to heat for 10 minutes before cooking.

2. Grill the corn and scallions until charred on all sides, 2 to 3 minutes for scallions, 4 to 5 minutes for corn, and then transfer them to a plate to cool slightly. Place the tomatoes in a grill basket and grill (shaking the basket for even charring) until they begin to blister, about 4 minutes.

3. Thinly slice the scallions and trim the corn kernels from the cob (the OXO Corn Stripper that Amanda Hesser gave me years ago makes quick work of this task). Add them to a bowl with the cilantro, lime juice, and a sprinkle of salt. Stir with a spatula to combine.

4. Cover a baking sheet with aluminum foil and arrange the tortilla chips in an even layer. Top with the corn mixture, black beans, cherry tomatoes, and cheeses. Place the baking sheet on the grill, close the grill, and cook until the cheese melts, about 4 minutes. Drizzle the nachos with crema and top with pickled peppers.

CONTINUED

Grilling Corn

The "right" way to grill corn (in the husk? silk removed? soaked in water or brine?) is one of those culinary quandaries that sparks contentious family riffs and Southern food symposium standoffs. Perhaps I'm exaggerating, but there are many opinions on the best way to get the job done. For instance, my husband passionately believes that corn in its husk should be soaked in water for at least 30 minutes before grilling, so it doesn't dry out over the fire. However, it's been documented that he once fed field corn (aka animal feed) to fellow exchange students in Sweden, so he cannot be fully trusted. I was raised amongst the verdant cornfields of Iowa, so I get to decide. The truth is, ears of sweet corn can be grilled in any way that allows the fire to either steam or directly char the kernels until they become tender and juicy. Ultimately, the most important issues are freshness (from the

second that fresh corn is picked, its sugars begin converting to chewier starches, so the sooner you eat it, the better) and the intensity of the heat you're dealing with. If you have a low fire and glowing embers, you can roast the corn in its husk—no need for soaking or removing silk—directly on the coals, turning the cob as needed for even cooking until the exterior is blackened and the kernels are steamy and tender. Removing the blackened husk creates a flurry of ash that might not be ideal for your dining room, but the distinctive, tamale-like flavor that it imparts is worth the mess. On most nights, and certainly for this book, I'm interested in the fastest and easiest approach, so I simply place the shucked, clean cobs over direct heat and use my tongs to rotate them until the kernels are evenly charred, creating a sweet, nutty flavor.

Cauliflower Steaks with Green Harissa

Serves 4

1 large head cauliflower

¼ cup (60ml) vegetable oil

Kosher salt and freshly ground black pepper

Green Harissa

2 tomatillos, husked and rinsed

½ onion, halved through the root

1 or 2 serrano chiles, as desired for heat

4 cloves garlic, unpeeled

2 cups (40g) fresh cilantro (leaves and tender stems)

2 cups (40g) fresh parsley (leaves and tender stems)

Large handful each of arugula and spinach

2 tablespoons white wine vinegar

1 teaspoon finely grated lemon zest

½ cup (120ml) olive oil

Kosher salt and freshly ground black pepper

Flaky salt

You can serve these "steaks" in any number of ways—topped with grilled bread crumbs (see page 21) with anchovies or over creamy feta or yogurt sauce, for instance—but I love how they play off spicy green harissa made with blistered tomatillos, serranos, and loads of aromatic herbs. This one's a grilled riff on the one served at Gjusta in Los Angeles and bound to be your new favorite condiment: Leftovers are delicious on sandwiches, with soft-cooked or crispy eggs, and as a marinade for chicken or shrimp.

1. Remove the leaves and trim the stem of the cauliflower, leaving the core intact. Place the cauliflower core-side down on a work surface. Starting in the center of the head, slice from top to bottom into four 1-inch (2.5cm) steaks. Place steaks on a rimmed baking sheet and any florets that break loose in a bowl. Drizzle the oil over the steaks and florets and generously season with kosher salt and pepper.

2. Prepare a charcoal grill for two-zone cooking and build a medium-high fire, or heat a gas grill to high. Carefully wipe the preheated grates with a lightly oiled paper towel. Using a grill brush, scrape the grill grates clean, then carefully wipe with a lightly oiled towel again. Allow a small cast-iron skillet or grill basket to heat for 5 minutes before cooking.

3. To make the harissa, blister the tomatillos, onion, chiles, and garlic in the preheated small cast-iron skillet or grill basket over direct heat, until charred and softened on all sides, 4 to 5 minutes for the tomatillos and chiles, a bit longer for the onion and garlic. Set aside to cool.

4. Stem and seed the chiles, peel the garlic, and place them both in a food processor. Add the tomatillos, cilantro, parsley, arugula and spinach, vinegar, lemon zest, and olive oil and puree until smooth. Season with salt and pepper.

5. Grill the cauliflower steaks (in a grill basket, if desired) over direct heat, rotating them around the fire as needed to prevent them from blackening before they're cooked, until deeply charred on the exterior and just tender at the core, 8 to 10 minutes per side. Grill any loose florets in a grill basket, tossing often, until browned and crispy, 5 to 7 minutes.

6. Serve the warm steaks on a pool of harissa and garnish with the crispy bits of florets and a sprinkle of flaky salt.

Smoky Ratatouille

Serves 4 to 6

¼ cup (60ml) extra-virgin olive oil, plus more for drizzling

1 red bell pepper—halved, cored, and seeded

1 yellow or orange bell pepper—halved, cored, and seeded

2 yellow squash (such as crookneck, pattypan, or zephyr), halved lengthwise

2 zucchini, halved lengthwise

4 Roma tomatoes, cored and halved lengthwise

Kosher salt and freshly ground black pepper

2 eggplants

2 small onions, unpeeled

2 large cloves garlic, minced, or 2 teaspoons Smoked Garlic (page 86)

Handful of fresh basil leaves

2 tablespoons freshly chopped marjoram or oregano

1 tablespoon red wine vinegar, plus more as desired

In the classic French preparation for ratatouille, summer vegetables are cooked separately so that each retains its optimal flavor and texture. This preparation uses the grill for a similar approach. Onions and eggplant are roasted directly on glowing embers so their flesh takes on a melting texture and smoky flavor. The bell peppers, squash, and tomatoes are charred on the hot grates so they retain a vibrant color and flavor. The smoky flavors of the ratatouille deepen overnight; serve leftovers topped with a poached or crispy egg, crumbled goat cheese, or grilled bread (see page 21) , or use it as a pizza topping (see page 36).

1. Prepare a charcoal grill for two-zone cooking and build a medium fire, or heat a gas grill to medium-high. Carefully wipe the preheated grates with a lightly oiled paper towel. Using a grill brush, scrape the grill grates clean, then carefully wipe with a lightly oiled towel again.

2. In a large bowl, combine the olive oil, bell peppers, yellow squash, zucchini, and tomatoes. Season generously with salt and pepper and toss to combine. Grill the vegetables over direct heat until charred on both sides, 6 to 10 minutes total.

3. Remove the grill grate; the coals should be covered with ash and glowing orangish red with no black remaining. Place the eggplants and onions directly on the coals and cook, using tongs to turn them occasionally, until skins are blackened and tender (and the eggplants have collapsed), 10 to 15 minutes for the eggplants, 20 to 25 for the onions.

4. Let the eggplants and onions cool slightly on a rimmed baking sheet. Cut the eggplant open lengthwise and use a spoon to scrape out the tender insides; discard the charred skin and stem. Place the eggplant flesh in a colander and let excess moisture drain for 15 to 30 minutes (as time allows).

5. Peel the onions, then chop the onions and eggplants and place them in a large bowl with the garlic. Dice the bell peppers, yellow squash, zucchini, and tomatoes and add to the bowl. Tear the basil leaves and add with the marjoram, vinegar, and a generous drizzle of olive oil. Season with salt and pepper and toss to combine. Taste and adjust seasonings and vinegar as desired. Serve warm or at room temperature.

Crispy Sweet Potatoes with Tiki Dressing & Sesame Seeds

Serves 4

4 sweet potatoes (preferably a mix of bright orange and pale cream-colored varieties)

Kosher salt

Tiki Dressing

5 tablespoons (75ml) soy sauce

5 tablespoons (75ml) Shaoxing rice wine

3 tablespoons fresh lime juice

2 tablespoons sugar

2 scallions, minced

3 tablespoons minced fresh ginger

2 cloves garlic, minced

Olive oil, for drizzling

Freshly ground black pepper

¼ cup (10g) freshly chopped cilantro (leaves and tender stems)

2 tablespoons toasted sesame seeds (preferably a mix of black and white)

I'd rather walk across a bed of hot coals than eat sweet potatoes covered with brown sugar and marshmallows. But I became a convert the first time I tasted sweet potatoes with a savory spin, simply roasted with olive oil and salt. Grilled sweet potatoes are even better because the heat caramelizes their natural sugars and tempers that sweetness with an appealingly acrid edge. To balance and brighten flavors, I love dressing the crispy rounds with this spicy, gingery dressing (packed with so many Asian ingredients that David and I gave it a Trader Vic's–style moniker), fresh cilantro, and crunchy toasted sesame seeds. To make this dish more substantial, serve the crispy potatoes warm or at room temperature over a bed of mixed greens, soba noodles, black Forbidden Rice, or quinoa.

1. Prepare a charcoal grill for two-zone cooking and build a medium-high fire, or heat a gas grill to high. Carefully wipe the preheated grates with a lightly oiled paper towel. Using a grill brush, scrape the grill grates clean, then carefully wipe with a lightly oiled towel again. If you're using a grill basket (a hinged basket is ideal here), allow it to heat for 10 minutes before cooking.

2. On the stove top, simmer the potatoes in generously salted water until just tender, about 12 minutes, and then drain and let cool.

3. Meanwhile, make the dressing. In a small bowl, whisk together the soy sauce, Shaoxing rice wine, lime juice, sugar, scallions, ginger, and garlic until blended and the sugar has dissolved.

4. When the sweet potatoes are cool enough to handle, peel and slice them into ½-inch (1.3cm) rounds. In a large bowl, drizzle the potatoes with enough olive oil to lightly coat, season with salt and pepper, and toss vigorously but carefully; you want the slices to remain intact, but you also want to rough up the edges to help them crisp up on the grill.

5. Place the potato rounds in 1 layer (in a hinged grill basket, if desired). Grill over direct heat, flipping and rotating the basket as needed for even charring, until the rounds are deeply browned and crisp, 3 to 4 minutes per side.

6. Transfer the potatoes to a serving platter, drizzle with the dressing, sprinkle with cilantro and sesame seeds, and serve.

Truckload of Marinated Vegetables

Serves 4, with leftovers

4 pounds (1.8kg) mixed vegetables (such as asparagus, broccolini, eggplant, endive, fennel, mushrooms, okra, onions, peppers, scallions, shallots, summer squash)

1¼ cups (300ml) extra-virgin olive oil

Kosher salt and freshly ground black pepper

¼ cup (60ml) white wine vinegar

¼ cup (10g) finely chopped fresh parsley

2 teaspoons freshly chopped marjoram or oregano

2 teaspoons freshly chopped thyme leaves

1 tablespoon Dijon mustard

1 tablespoon finely grated lemon zest

2 cloves garlic, thinly sliced

Generous pinch of dried red chile (such as chopped piquín, arbol, or red pepper flakes)

Invest about an hour grilling vegetables (on Sunday afternoon, perhaps?) and you'll be rewarded with several days of stellar sandwiches, taco fillings, quick and nourishing pasta or grain combinations, and more. The searing heat of a live fire adds intrigue to raw vegetables—their natural sugars intensify, streaks of char add moxie, and textures become tender and luscious. The following approach works for anything you want to grill and leaves you with a happy heap of vegetables, which actually improve as they marinate in a fragrant bath of olive oil, vinegar, and fresh herbs. For a punched-up flavor, add capers, pickled chiles, olives, or dried red chiles to the marinade.

For the best results, halve or slice larger vegetables and keep smaller varieties (broccolini, asparagus, baby squash) whole. The more surface area you expose to the grill, the quicker the vegetable will cook and the more flavor you'll impart. After cooking, you can chop them however you please. Make sure that all the vegetables are thoroughly washed *and* dried—excess moisture will create steam, which inhibits the charring process.

1. Prepare a charcoal grill for two-zone cooking and build a medium-high fire, or heat a gas grill to high. Carefully wipe the preheated grates with a lightly oiled paper towel. Using a grill brush, scrape the grill grates clean, then carefully wipe with a lightly oiled towel again.

2. Depending on the vegetables you're using, slice them into rounds, halve them, or leave them whole and then combine them in a large bowl. Drizzle with ¼ cup (60ml) of the olive oil, season generously with salt and pepper, and toss to evenly coat. Set aside while the grill heats, tossing occasionally.

3. In a medium bowl, whisk together the vinegar, parsley, marjoram, thyme, Dijon, lemon zest, garlic, red chile, and the remaining cup (240ml) of olive oil. Season with salt and pepper.

4. Working in batches if necessary, grill the vegetables in a single layer over direct heat, turning and rotating as needed for even cooking, until charred and slightly tender (2 to 3 minutes for small, skinny vegetables; 4 to 5 minutes for larger, denser pieces). Chop or slice the vegetables as desired, transfer to the marinade, and toss gently to combine. Serve immediately, or let the mixture marinate at room temperature for up to 3 hours or refrigerate in a sealed container for up to 4 days.

Grilled Vegetable Sandwiches

Grilled vegetable sandwiches are endlessly versatile and can be made with anything that inspires you at the farmers' market. The essentials, in my book, are well-seasoned vegetables; a vibrant condiment like green or black olive tapenade, pesto, or Green Harissa (page 95); cheese that melds the ingredients together (fresh mozzarella, chèvre, feta); and a sturdy, crusty bread or roll that soaks up the flavorful marinade.

Grilled Mushroom Bánh Mì

Serves 4

Vietnamese Marinade

1 bunch cilantro (leaves and tender stems)

1 bunch scallions, trimmed and cut into thirds

2 serrano chiles, stemmed and seeded

¼ cup (60ml) fish sauce (preferably Red Boat)

¼ cup (60ml) fresh lime juice

2 garlic cloves

¼ wheel palm sugar or 2 tablespoons coconut sugar or turbinado sugar

3 pounds (1.4kg) mixed mushrooms (any combination of cremini, portobello, porcini, or shiitake), stemmed

4 French rolls, split

Sriracha-spiked mayonnaise

Crunchy accompaniments of choice (such as julienned carrots, shaved radishes, lettuce leaves like frisée or Bibb, and cilantro sprigs)

Chris Shepherd's acclaimed restaurant Underbelly is a love letter to the cultural diversity of Houston, which has one of the largest Vietnamese populations in the country. As a result, fish sauce has become his favorite go-to flavor enhancer (he goes through 5 gallons a week). Chris uses this Vietnamese-style marinade for pork collar, but it's also delicious with mushrooms (bonus: they absorb the vibrant flavors in just 30 minutes). A slather of sriracha-spiked mayo and a stack of fresh, crunchy garnishes like radishes, carrots, and lettuce are the perfect balance to the smoky flavor of the grilled mushrooms. Just add a toasted bun and a cold beer.

1. To make the marinade, puree the cilantro, scallions, chiles, fish sauce, lime juice, garlic, and sugar in a blender until smooth.

2. Place the mushrooms in a baking dish, pour over the marinade, and toss to combine. Marinate at room temperature for 30 minutes.

3. Prepare a charcoal grill for two-zone cooking and build a medium-high fire, or heat a gas grill to high. Carefully wipe the preheated grates with a lightly oiled paper towel. Using a grill brush, scrape the grill grates clean, then carefully wipe with a lightly oiled towel again. If you're using a grill basket, allow it to heat for 10 minutes before cooking.

4. Grill the mushrooms (in the grill basket or directly on the grates) over direct heat until charred on both sides, about 5 minutes. Transfer to a plate to cool slightly. Grill the French rolls over direct heat, cut side down, until lightly toasted, about a minute.

5. To assemble the sandwiches, spread a generous amount of sriracha mayo on the bottom half of rolls. Divide the warm mushrooms among the rolls and top with the carrots, radishes, lettuce, and cilantro sprigs as desired. Cover with the top half of the rolls and gently press the sandwich together to meld.

Smoky Tomato & Red Lentil Soup

Serves 6 to 8

6 plum tomatoes, halved
lengthwise

1 large onion, quartered
through the root

1½-inch (4cm) knob
fresh ginger, peeled and
coarsely chopped

2 cloves garlic, peeled
and coarsely chopped,
or 2 teaspoons Smoked
Garlic (page 86)

2 tablespoons vegetable oil

1 to 2 tablespoons red
curry paste

1 teaspoon ground cumin

1 teaspoon ground
coriander

2 cups (380g) dried red
lentils, rinsed

4 cups (950ml) water or
chicken stock

One 13.5-ounce (398ml)
can full-fat coconut milk

Kosher salt and freshly
ground black pepper

Fresh cilantro leaves

Juice from 1 fresh or
grilled lime

This fragrant soup is worth firing up the grill for, but it's also a super-easy meal to prep after you've grilled something else (the soup will keep up to 5 days in the fridge). Plum tomatoes and onion are charred on the hot grates, then pureed to create a smoky base. Red curry paste, ginger, and coconut milk join red lentils to create a nourishing soup with a rich, velvety texture. To create a heartier version of this soup, sometimes I make this recipe with half red lentils and half yellow split peas. Serve with steamed rice, if desired, and a squeeze of fresh or grilled lime juice.

1. Prepare a charcoal grill for two-zone cooking and build a medium fire, or heat a gas grill to medium-high. Carefully wipe the preheated grates with a lightly oiled paper towel. Using a grill brush, scrape the grill grates clean, then carefully wipe with a lightly oiled towel again. If you're using a grill basket, allow it to heat for 10 minutes before cooking.

2. Grill the tomatoes and onion over direct heat until evenly charred, turning and rotating as needed for even cooking, 4 to 5 minutes. Let cool, then refrigerate until needed or proceed with making the soup.

3. In a blender, puree the ginger and garlic with the tomato-onion mixture, including any juices, until mostly smooth.

4. On the stove top, heat the vegetable oil in a 4-quart (3.8L) heavy pot over medium-high heat. When the oil shimmers, add the red curry paste, cumin, and coriander and cook, stirring, until fragrant and combined, about 3 minutes. Add the tomato-onion mixture, stir to combine, then add the lentils, water, and coconut milk and bring mixture to a boil. Lower the heat and simmer until thickened and the lentils are cooked, about 25 minutes. Season with salt and pepper and garnish with cilantro and a drizzle of lime juice.

Fresh Catches

Basic Grilled Fish with Grilled Vegetable Vinaigrette

Serves 4

Grilled Vegetable Vinaigrette

1 fennel bulb, trimmed

1 small red onion

1 small head Treviso or other radicchio

½ cup (120ml) extra-virgin olive oil

3 tablespoons sherry vinegar

1 teaspoon flaky salt

1 small clove garlic, minced

2 tablespoons capers

2 or 3 crumbled dried piquín chiles or generous pinch red pepper flakes

¼ cup (10g) coarsely chopped fresh mint or parsley leaves

¼ cup (10g) coarsely chopped fresh marjoram or oregano leaves

Four 6-ounce (170g) center-cut halibut, sea bass, or swordfish steaks (about ¾ inch/2cm thick)

Extra-virgin olive oil, for drizzling

Kosher salt

Freshly ground black pepper

Flaky salt

1 lemon, cut into wedges

With a firm texture and high oil content, meaty steaks of tuna, mahi mahi, and swordfish are particularly well suited to grilling, but I also enjoy halibut or sea bass in this preparation. Brushing both the fish and the grill with oil (and using a slotted fish spatula) will make the steaks easier to flip. The simple beauty of a lightly charred fresh catch needs little more than a squeeze of lemon and a sprinkle of salt, but I also love serving grilled fish with Tomatillo Salsa (page 151), Sumac Yogurt Sauce (page 176), and this pleasingly bitter and herbaceous vinaigrette inspired by one in April Bloomfield's cookbook *A Girl and Her Greens*. Use it on grilled bread, eggs fried in olive oil, and crisp rounds of grilled potatoes (opposite), too.

1. Prepare a charcoal grill for two-zone cooking and build a medium fire, or heat a gas grill to medium-high. Carefully wipe the preheated grill grates with a lightly oiled paper towel. Using a grill brush, scrape the grill grates clean, then carefully wipe with a lightly oiled towel again.

2. To make the vinaigrette, halve the fennel bulb lengthwise and cut each half into approximately 1-inch (2.5cm) wedges, keeping the root intact to help the wedges hold together on the grill. Cut the onion into ½-inch (1.3cm) rounds. Quarter the radicchio, keeping the stem intact.

3. Grill the fennel, onion, and radicchio over direct heat, turning and rotating as needed for even cooking, until the fennel and onion are lightly charred and cooked through but still have a little bite, about 20 minutes. The radicchio is ready when the leaves are wilted, the tips crackly, and the color has changed from magenta to sienna with dark brown edges, 15 to 20 minutes.

4. As they finish, pop the grilled vegetables into a bowl and cover with plastic wrap. Once fully cool, chop the vegetables into roughly ½-inch (1.3cm) pieces.

5. In the same bowl, stir together the vegetables, oil, vinegar, flaky salt, garlic, capers, and chiles. Stir in the mint and marjoram. On a baking sheet or large plate, brush or drizzle each steak with 2 teaspoons olive oil and season generously with kosher salt on both sides. Carefully place the fish on the grill over direct heat. Cook 3 to 4 minutes per side for medium-rare, 120°F to 125°F (49°C to 52°C).

6. Use a spatula to transfer the fish to a serving dish. Top with the vinaigrette, lightly drizzle with olive oil, sprinkle with pepper and flaky salt, and serve alongside lemon wedges.

Crispy Octopus & Potatoes

Serves 4

1 cleaned whole octopus (2½ to 3 pounds/1.1 to 1.4kg)

1 onion, peeled and halved

1 head garlic, unpeeled and halved crosswise

3 lemons, halved

3 or 4 fresh bay leaves

1 teaspoon peppercorns

Kosher salt and freshly ground black pepper

2 to 3 cups (475 to 710ml) dry white wine

Extra-virgin olive oil, for drizzling

4 large Yukon gold potatoes

Freshly chopped parsley

I brought my kids along to the fish market and was prepared for shrieks of protest. After all, an uncooked octopus can be an alarming sight at the seafood counter—reminiscent of an ouzo-soaked cruise through the Mediterranean, perhaps, but not necessarily the makings of family dinner. That shouldn't be the case, because grilling up crisp, tender sections of octopus is easier than you think. Much to my surprise, the kids had great fun picking out our specimen. To achieve a tender texture, it's essential to poach octopus for 45 minutes before grilling (the good news is this can be done a day in advance). Crispy rounds of grilled potatoes are the perfect earthy foil for the tender mollusk. Aioli would be a delicious addition, too, but I usually just rely on a generous drizzle of quality olive oil and a squeeze of lemon.

1. On the stove top in a large pot, combine the octopus, onion, garlic, 2 lemon halves, bay leaves, peppercorns, and 1 tablespoon salt. Pour in the white wine, then the same amount of water, plus more as needed to cover the octopus. Bring to a boil over medium-high heat, then lower the heat and simmer, partially covered, until tender, 30 to 45 minutes. To test doneness, insert a sharp knife into the thickest part of the octopus (the skirt, where the head meets the legs); it should yield with a little resistance, like a cooked potato. Drain, discarding everything but the octopus, and set aside or cover and refrigerate for up to a day.

2. If you chilled the octopus, about an hour before grilling, remove it from the fridge. Slice it into manageable serving pieces that will be easy to eat with the potatoes—tentacles about 4-inch (10cm) lengths, head halved or quartered—and drizzle with enough olive oil to lightly coat, season with salt and pepper, and gently toss.

3. On the stove top, simmer the potatoes in generously salted water until tender, about 15 minutes, then drain and let cool (the potatoes can also be cooked in a separate pot while the octopus poaches). When they're cool enough to handle, peel and slice them into ½-inch (1.3cm) rounds. Drizzle the potatoes with enough olive oil to lightly coat, season with salt and pepper, and toss carefully but somewhat vigorously; you want the slices to remain intact but you also want to rough up the edges to help them crisp up on the grill.

CONTINUED

4. Prepare a charcoal grill for two-zone cooking and build a medium-high fire, or heat a gas grill to high. Carefully wipe the preheated grates with a lightly oiled paper towel. Using a grill brush, scrape the grill grates clean, then carefully wipe with a lightly oiled towel again. Heat a grill basket (preferably hinged) for 10 minutes before cooking.

5. Place the potato rounds in 1 layer in the grill basket. Grill over direct heat, flipping and rotating the basket as needed for even charring, until the rounds are charred and crispy, 5 to 6 minutes. Transfer the potatoes to a serving platter.

6. Grill the octopus over direct heat until nicely charred and browned, turning and rotating as needed for even cooking, 10 to 12 minutes. When fully cooked, the suction cups should feel dry and crisp, not fleshy.

7. Transfer the warm octopus to a bowl, toss with additional olive oil and the lemon juice from the remaining 2 lemons, and season with salt and pepper. Serve over the grilled potatoes, drizzling with additional olive oil as desired, and sprinkle with parsley.

Instant Vacation Swordfish Skewers

Serves 4

2 to 2¼ pounds (900g to 1kg) swordfish fillets or another firm white fish (such as halibut, monkfish, or sea bass)

Olive oil, for drizzling

Kosher salt and freshly ground black pepper

1 large lemon, sliced into half-moons, plus more for serving

8 to 10 fresh bay leaves

2 tablespoons freshly chopped oregano

1 tablespoon freshly chopped dill

Pinch of red pepper flakes

Flaky salt

Several years ago, I spent time cooking at a Franco-American arts foundation in a château in the south of France—and all sorts of European food adventures were within striking distance. One of the highlights was meeting my parents in Athens, where my dad had been stationed in the Air Force. Among my favorite memories from that trip: the rich, deep voice of the man who ran our hotel in the Plaka, his advice that basement restaurants are much better than those with tables on a pretty courtyard (the former can't get by on their view), and stunning skewers of grilled swordfish at every turn. When I'm pining for salt spray and sunshine, pairing fresh fish with a charcoal fire provides an instant vacation. You can serve these skewers over lemony orzo and crumbled feta or with grilled pita bread and tzatziki. Because they're so much leaner than meat, flipping fish kebabs can be daunting. I find it's easier if I carefully loosen the fish with a metal fish spatula (to preserve the delicious browned crust) before lifting the skewers from the grates.

1. Prepare a charcoal grill for two-zone grilling and build a medium-high fire, or heat a gas grill to high. Carefully wipe the preheated grill grates with a lightly oiled paper towel. Using a grill brush, scrape the grill grates clean, then carefully wipe with a lightly oiled towel again.

2. Slice the fish into even 2-inch (5cm) chunks. In a bowl, drizzle the fish with enough olive oil to generously coat and season them with kosher salt and black pepper. Add the lemon, bay leaves, oregano, dill, and red pepper flakes and gently toss to combine.

3. Divide the fish, lemon, and bay leaves among 4 skewers and grill over direct heat, turning as needed for even cooking, until lightly browned, charred, and cooked through, 10 to 12 minutes. Serve with lemons and a sprinkle of flaky salt.

Choose the Right Skewer

Metal skewers are sturdy and reusable, but they retain a lot of heat, so they're not ideal to transfer to the table. For that reason, I almost always use bamboo skewers that have been soaked in water for 30 minutes.

Beach House Pasta with Shrimp & Grilled Limes

Serves 4 to 6

2 pounds (900g) medium shrimp, peeled and deveined with tails intact

Extra-virgin olive oil, for drizzling

Kosher salt and freshly ground black pepper

2 limes

1 pound (450g) spaghetti

½ cup (120ml) crème fraîche

2 tablespoons freshly chopped tarragon or chives

3 tablespoons freshly chopped parsley

Red pepper flakes

Flaky salt

This is the perfect, easy-breezy meal because it can be assembled in the time it takes for the pasta to boil. The components are simple, but the charred flavor of the grilled sweet shrimp and limes adds delicious depth. Once you start cooking, this dish comes together quickly, so make sure you have the rest of the meal ready to go (though all you really need is some wine, chilled). You can also use half the amount of shrimp and add a pound (450g) of scallops, just be sure to sauté them separately; they'll brown and crisp better if they have more room to cook.

1. Prepare a charcoal grill for two-zone cooking and build a medium-high fire, or heat a gas grill to high. Carefully wipe the preheated grill grates with a lightly oiled paper towel. Using a grill brush, scrape the grill grates clean, then carefully wipe with a lightly oiled towel again. If you're using a grill basket or pan, allow it to heat for 10 minutes before cooking.

2. In a large bowl, drizzle the shrimp with enough olive oil to lightly coat, season with kosher salt and pepper, and toss to combine.

3. On the stove top, bring a large pot of salted water to a boil. While the water heats, zest the limes and then slice them in half lengthwise. Add the pasta and cook until al dente per the package directions. Reserve 1 cup (240ml) of the pasta water and then drain the pasta.

4. Grill the shrimp and limes over direct heat, stirring and flipping with tongs until the shrimp are evenly cooked (about 4 minutes) and the limes are slashed with grill marks, 2 to 3 minutes. Let cool on a rimmed baking sheet.

5. In a large bowl, gently toss the shrimp, cooked pasta, lime zest, crème fraîche, tarragon, and parsley to combine. Season with salt and pepper, add a generous drizzle of olive oil, and toss again; add a splash of the reserved pasta water if needed to create a creamy texture. Serve immediately in warmed bowls with a squeeze of grilled lime, some red pepper flakes, additional black pepper, and a sprinkle of flaky salt.

Gulf Coast Shrimp Tacos

Serves 4

3 tablespoons olive oil

2 tablespoons fresh lime juice

2 chipotle peppers in adobo sauce

2 cloves garlic, minced, or 2 teaspoons Smoked Garlic (page 86)

Kosher salt and freshly ground black pepper

2 pounds (900g) medium or large shrimp (preferably Gulf), peeled and deveined with tails removed

Slaw

½ head napa cabbage, thinly sliced or shredded

½ head red cabbage, thinly sliced or shredded

2 large carrots, peeled and shredded

Leaves from 1 small bunch cilantro, coarsely chopped

¼ cup (55g) mayonnaise

2 tablespoons fresh lime juice

¼ cup (60ml) olive oil

Kosher salt and freshly ground black pepper

2 tablespoons hot sauce (preferably Crystal or Cholula), plus more for serving

8 to 10 corn tortillas

Lime wedges

Here in Austin, where a favorite restaurant marquee reads "Body by Queso," it's not uncommon to have tacos three times a day. The routine isn't as strange or repetitive as it sounds, because it's easy to have an entirely different experience at each meal. For instance, I might have egg-and-chorizo tacos for breakfast, a brisket taco for lunch, and this spicy, refreshing combination for dinner. The confluence of lightly charred shrimp with crunchy cabbage slaw and an audacious amount of hot sauce is my idea of the perfect warm-weather meal. Seek out the best-quality corn tortillas you can find—when you open the package, you should be hit with the earthy aroma of fresh masa. And because you can eat anything in a tortilla, consider blazing a new path and pairing this shrimp with the corn and zucchini mixture in Queso Panela Tacos (page 48); or refried black beans, grated Cotija, and Tomatillo Salsa (page 151); or Celery Root Remoulade (page 180).

1. In a food processor or blender, puree the olive oil, lime juice, chipotles, garlic, 1 teaspoon salt, and ½ teaspoon black pepper until smooth. Pour the mixture into a resealable plastic bag. Add the shrimp and use your hands to coat the shrimp. Seal the bag, pressing out the air, and set aside to marinate at room temperature while you heat the grill or refrigerate for up to a day.

2. Prepare a charcoal grill for two-zone cooking and build a medium-high fire, or heat a gas grill to high. Carefully wipe the preheated grill grates with a lightly oiled paper towel. Using a grill brush, scrape the grill grates clean, then carefully wipe with a lightly oiled towel again. If you're using a grill basket, allow it to heat for 10 minutes before cooking.

3. To make the slaw, in a large bowl, toss together the cabbages, carrots, cilantro, mayo, lime juice, and olive oil to combine. Season with salt, pepper, and hot sauce and toss again, then taste and adjust the seasoning as desired (adding more lime juice, mayo, or other seasonings). Set aside or refrigerate for up to a day.

4. Remove the shrimp from the marinade and grill over direct heat, stirring and flipping them with tongs until evenly cooked, about 4 minutes. Transfer the shrimp to a serving bowl and cover with aluminum foil to keep warm.

5. Grill the tortillas over direct heat until lightly charred, about 30 seconds per side. Keep warm in a basket or wrapped in a kitchen towel. Serve with the grilled shrimp, cabbage slaw, additional hot sauce, and lime wedges on the side.

Herb-Basted Smoked Salmon

Serves 6 to 8

2 cups (180g) wood chips (preferably applewood or cherrywood)

One 4-pound (1.8kg) skin-on salmon fillet, pinbones removed

Kosher salt and freshly ground black pepper

2 sprigs marjoram

2 sprigs thyme

2 sprigs dill

3 to 4 tablespoons (45 to 60ml) olive oil

Flaky salt

Lemon wedges

A grilled side of salmon makes an impressive centerpiece for a dinner party or lavish brunch. Adding wood chips to the glowing embers infuses the fish with a fantastic smoky flavor in a surprisingly short time, and basting the salmon with an herb sprig dipped in olive oil adds an additional layer of flavor. While you could place the salmon right on the grill, aluminum foil makes it easier to rotate the salmon to ensure even doneness (a necessary step since the large fillet tends to stretch into both temperature zones) and remove from the grill (meaning the skin won't stick and your grill will stay clean). The rich flavor of the salmon needs nothing more than a sprinkle of flaky salt, but you can also serve it with lemon halves. To round out the meal, add crispy rounds of grilled potatoes (see page 113) or grilled bread, a shaved radish salad, and/or a salad of young, tender lettuces. Use leftovers to make tacos with a spicy red cabbage slaw (see page 121).

1. Soak the wood chips in water for 30 minutes.

2. Prepare a charcoal grill for two-zone cooking and build a medium-high fire, or heat a gas grill to high. Carefully wipe the preheated grill grates with a lightly oiled paper towel. Using a grill brush, scrape the grill grates clean, then carefully wipe with a lightly oiled towel again.

3. Measure out 2 sheets of aluminum foil that are 12 inches (30cm) longer than the salmon and put them on a rimless baking sheet. Place the salmon skin side down on the foil and generously season with kosher salt and pepper.

4. Drain the wood chips and scatter them over the coals. If using a gas grill, put them in a perforated aluminum foil packet or smoker box and place directly over the flames. Secure the stems of the marjoram, thyme, and dill sprigs with kitchen twine to form a basting brush (see photo on page 125). Pour the olive oil into a small bowl.

5. Using the short ends of the foil as handles, carefully slide the fish off the baking sheet and onto the grill over indirect heat, adjusting as needed. Close the grill, vent appropriately for indirect cooking, and cook until the salmon is just cooked through and opaque in the center, about 30 minutes, dipping the herb brush in oil and basting the salmon every 10 minutes (do this quickly so the grill isn't open for too long). When the salmon is cooked, carefully slide the fish back onto the baking sheet and let rest for at least 10 minutes. Season with flaky salt, lemons, and pepper.

Grilled Branzino with Thai Basil Butter

Serves 4

Four 1-pound (450g)
or two 2-pound (900g)
whole branzino or another
white fish (such as sea
bass, loup de mer, or
porgy), scaled and gutted

Kosher salt and freshly
ground black pepper

¼ cup (60g) unsalted
butter, at room
temperature

Leaves from 2 or 3 sprigs
Thai basil

Thin slices of lemon or
lime, garlic cloves, peeled
ginger, and jalapeños for
stuffing (you'll want 2 or
3 slices of each per fish)

Extra-virgin olive oil,
for rubbing and drizzling

Lemon wedges

Flaky salt

Whether it's a massive red snapper or a branzino for one, grilled whole fish—with delicious crispy skin and flaky meat—is a thing of beauty that's surprisingly easy to pull off. To set yourself up for success, start by seeking out the freshest fish you can find and ask the fishmonger to scale and gut the fish for you. The most daunting part of the process is flipping the fish, but that's easy if you properly prepare the grill (preheat, clean, oil) and the fish (allow it to come to room temperature, dry, oil). You can round out the meal with steamed rice, a simple cucumber salad, or simply grilled bread.

1. About 30 minutes before grilling, remove the fish from the fridge and let it come to room temperature.

2. Prepare a charcoal grill for two-zone cooking and build a medium-high fire, or heat a gas grill to high. Carefully wipe the preheated grill grates with a lightly oiled paper towel. Using a grill brush, scrape the grill grates clean, then carefully wipe with a lightly oiled towel again.

3. Thoroughly pat the fish dry with paper towels. Generously season inside and out with kosher salt and pepper. Vigorously stir together the butter and whole Thai basil leaves to combine—you want to agitate the basil leaves so they release their perfume.

4. Smear 1 or 2 tablespoons of the basil butter in the cavity of each fish, then stuff in the lemon, garlic, ginger, and jalapeño. Use your hands or a pastry brush to coat the exterior of the fish with olive oil. If the cavity is bursting, secure it by tying kitchen twine around the middle of the fish.

5. Grill the fish over direct heat until the bottom is browned, about 5 minutes. Using a carving fork, insert the tines between the grill grate and the fish. Carefully attempt to lift the fish from below; if it resists, cook the fish for 1 minute more, then try again. When the fish separates easily from grill, use a spatula to turn it onto the other side. Cook until an instant-read thermometer inserted in the thickest part registers 135°F (57°C), about 5 minutes longer. If the skin begins to char before the fish is cooked through, transfer the fish to the cooler side of the grill to finish cooking.

6. Remove the fish from the grill and let rest for 5 minutes. Serve smaller fish as individual servings. For larger fish, insert a thin fillet knife behind the head and run it between the flesh and the bones to lift off the fillet. Turn the fish over and repeat. Serve on a platter with lemon wedges and flaky salt.

Salt-Crusted Snapper with Spicy Fish Sauce Vinaigrette

Serves 2 to 4

One 4- to 5-pound (1.8 to 2.3kg) whole red snapper, tilapia, or porgy, scaled and gutted

1 large stalk lemongrass, bottom trimmed, outer layers removed

2 cups (360g) kosher salt

1 large egg white, beaten

½ cup (120ml) Spicy Fish Sauce Vinaigrette (page 87)

Crusting an entire fish in a salt crust seems like a leap of faith, or perhaps a party trick, but consider this recipe your gateway to grilling whole fish—the tender, flaky result will have you hooked. As the fish grills, the crust firms and creates a buffer from the heat, so it preserves moisture, prevents overcooking, and provides the distinct flavor of a fire. For the best results, it's important to ensure that the fish is completely dry before brushing it with egg white, which acts as glue for the salt. Serve with Spicy Fish Sauce Vinaigrette (an addictive condiment that can be made well in advance, or right before you cook the fish) and steamed jasmine rice, if desired.

1. Thoroughly pat the fish dry with paper towels. Using a meat pounder or heavy skillet, whack the thick end of the lemongrass a few times to bruise it, which helps release its aromatic oils. Insert the stalk through the fish's belly so that the thin end comes out of the fish's mouth (you may need to use a thin slicing knife to clear a path from belly to mouth) and tuck the thick end into the belly until it's no longer visible.

2. Spread the salt on a rimmed baking sheet. Using a brush or your hands, coat 1 side of the fish with a thin layer of the beaten egg white. Lay the fish, egg white–brushed side down, onto the bed of salt, gently pressing down on the fish so the salt adheres. Brush the other side with egg white (there's no need to use it all), flip the fish over, and use your hands to pat the salt on the fish to form an even layer that's approximately ¼ inch (6mm) thick—it should be just thick enough to partially obscure the color of the snapper. Flip the fish once more and do the same on the other side (there will be a lot of salt left over).

3. Prepare a charcoal grill for one-zone cooking and build a medium-high fire, or heat a gas grill to high. Carefully wipe the preheated grill grates with a lightly oiled paper towel. Using a grill brush, scrape the grill grates clean, then carefully wipe with a lightly oiled towel again.

4. Grill the fish with the lid closed for at least 6 minutes to allow the crust to firm, and then begin checking the underside. When the crust is a light golden brown with a few darker brown patches, use the spatula and a pair of tongs to carefully flip it. Continue to cook, with the grill covered, until both sides are golden brown and the fish is just cooked through to the bone, and a thermometer inserted into the flesh at the thickest part of the fish (behind the head at the fish's back) registers 125°F (52°C), 16 to 20 minutes. Transfer to a platter.

5. Using the tip of a sharp knife, score the salt crust, once across each side (starting at the tail and cutting horizontally toward the gills) and once across the midsection. Peel back the skin in 1 piece, and then repeat on the other side of the fish; discard both pieces or leave them on the plate as garnish. Use a slicing knife and a serving spatula to portion the fish into servings and serve warm with a bowl of the vinaigrette.

For Easier Flipping, Use a Fork Lift

Using a two-pronged carving fork to lift the fish from the cooking grate is a smart way to gauge doneness. If the fish sticks to the grate, it needs more time over the heat. Wait until you can tease the fish up and off the grate without the skin sticking and tearing.

One-Pot Clambake

Serves 4 to 6

2 cups (180g) wood chips
(preferably fruitwood
or hickory)

1 pound (450g) andouille
sausage, cut into 2-inch
(5cm) lengths

2 pounds (900g) small
new potatoes, scrubbed
and halved

1 fennel bulb, cored
and thinly sliced

4 cloves garlic, crushed
and unpeeled

2 or 3 sprigs parsley

4 fresh bay leaves

Two 12-ounce (355ml)
beers or 3 cups (710ml)
water

2 teaspoons Old Bay
seasoning

4 ears corn, shucked
and cut into quarters

4 pounds (1.8kg) littleneck
clams, scrubbed

Melted butter

Lemon halves

In an ideal world, clambakes include a beach and a sunset, but you don't need a stretch of coast or a fire pit in the sand to enjoy the quintessential summer feast of sausage, clams, potatoes, corn, and butter. The key to this cooking process is layering the ingredients so the heftier sausage and potatoes are on the bottom to diffuse the direct heat and avoid overcooking the clams.

1. Soak the wood chips in water for 30 minutes.

2. Prepare a charcoal grill for two-zone cooking and build a medium-high fire, or heat a gas grill to high. Carefully wipe the preheated grill grates with a lightly oiled paper towel. Using a grill brush, scrape the grill grates clean, then carefully wipe with a lightly oiled towel again.

3. Line a roasting pan (or a wide pot that fits inside the closed grill) with the sausage, potatoes, fennel, garlic, parsley, and bay leaves and just enough beer or water (or a combination of the two) to cover the ingredients. Loosely cover the pan with aluminum foil—don't make a tight seal, because you want the smoky flavor of the fire to be absorbed. Drain the wood chips and scatter them over the coals. If using a gas grill, put them in a perforated aluminum foil packet or smoker box and place directly over the flames. Carefully place the pan on the grate over direct heat, close the lid, and allow the mixture to come to a lively simmer. (You can also put the pot right in the coals.) Continue to simmer, checking on the strength of the simmer and adjusting vents or rotating the pan as needed for even cooking, until the potatoes are tender, about 20 minutes.

4. Sprinkle the Old Bay over the potatoes, top with the corn and clams, cover the grill, and cook until the clams open wide and the corn is cooked through, about 10 minutes.

5. Use a slotted spoon to transfer the clambake onto newspaper-lined tables and serve with melted butter and lemon halves.

Seafood Paella with Freekeh & Lima Beans

Serves 6 to 8

4 cups (950ml) chicken
stock

2 cups (475ml) fish stock
or clam broth

¼ teaspoon saffron
threads

¼ cup (60ml) olive oil

12 ounces (340g)
Spanish chorizo, halved
lengthwise and crosswise

1 onion, finely chopped

1 red bell pepper, seeded
and finely chopped

3 cloves garlic,
thinly sliced

½ teaspoon smoked
paprika

2¼ cups (515g) freekeh
or bomba, arborio, or
Calasparra rice

8 large head-on shrimp

1 pound (450g) littleneck
clams, scrubbed

8 ounces (225g) mussels,
scrubbed

1 cup (160g) frozen
Fordhook lima beans,
thawed

Handful of haricots
verts, halved

Freshly chopped parsley

Hot sauce

If there's ever a reason to make Grilled Pineapple Punch (page 17) and invite friends over for a feast, it's paella on the grill. The key to a stress-free meal is having your ingredients prepped before you strike a match so you can use the fire to its best advantage. Paella is a lifetime pursuit, so even if you don't nail the perfect socarrat (rice that gets caramelized and crusty on the bottom of the pan) the first time, your game will improve each time you make it.

1. On the stove top, bring the chicken stock, fish stock, and saffron to a simmer over medium-high heat; remove from heat and set aside to steep.

2. Prepare a charcoal grill for one-zone cooking and build a medium-high fire, or heat a gas grill to high. Carefully wipe the preheated grill grates with a lightly oiled paper towel. Using a grill brush, scrape the grill grates clean, then carefully wipe with a lightly oiled towel again.

3. Place a 15-inch (38cm) paella pan or large enameled cast-iron casserole on the grill grate over direct heat and pour in the olive oil. Return the stock mixture to a simmer over medium-high heat (if your gas grill has a side burner, you can do this outside). Add the chorizo to the paella pan and cook until nicely browned, 3 to 4 minutes. Remove with a slotted spoon and set aside.

4. Add the onion and bell pepper and cook until softened, stirring occasionally, about 5 minutes. Add the garlic and paprika and cook until fragrant, about 2 minutes. Add the freekeh and cook, stirring, until it is evenly coated in the oil, about 1 minute. Add 4 cups (950ml) of the hot stock, stir the freekeh once, and spread it into an even layer in the pan. Close the grill and cook, stirring only when necessary for even cooking, until half of the liquid is absorbed, about 10 minutes for freekeh, 15 minutes for rice.

5. Add the remaining stock and nestle the chorizo and shrimp into the freekeh, followed by the clams and mussels, hinge side down. Continue to cook, flipping the shrimp halfway through, until the shrimp and shellfish are cooked through, the clams and mussels open wide, and the liquid is absorbed, 10 to 15 minutes. Scatter the lima beans and haricots verts on top, close the grill, and cook for 5 minutes more. Remove from heat and allow the paella to stand 10 minutes before serving.

6. Scatter with parsley and serve the paella warm, straight from the pan using a large metal spoon to scrape up any socarrat (crunchy crust) from the bottom. Pass the hot sauce.

Barbecued Birds
& Juicy Pork

Party Wings with Cholula Butter

Serves 4

3 pounds (1.4kg) chicken wing drumettes

Olive oil, for drizzling

Kosher salt and freshly ground black pepper

¼ cup (60ml) Cholula hot sauce

3 tablespoons freshly chopped parsley

2 tablespoons unsalted butter, at room temperature

2 tablespoons fresh lemon juice

2 cloves garlic, minced

I wasn't a wing enthusiast until I cooked them on the grill—then I was hooked. The high heat renders the fat, crisping the skin and making them taste both rich and improbably light (unlike the gut-bomb sports bar variety). Of course, wings are the quintessential party snack, something spicy and messy to entertain you while you're sipping cocktails and swapping one-liners. They can also be the attraction, join other small plates, or provide a hearty snack for friends waiting on something with a longer cooking time, like a smoked whole turkey or brisket. A two-zone fire is essential here because it provides nice heat for an initial char, as well as a moderate zone to cook the meat through without scorching the skin. I use drumettes because they're meaty and easier to eat, and Cholula for the hot sauce. It's a smoky Mexican hot sauce that's delicious on eggs, tacos, and just about everything. For more sauce ideas, though, flip the page.

1. Place the drumettes in a large bowl, drizzle with enough olive oil to lightly coat, generously season with salt and pepper, and toss to combine.

2. Prepare a charcoal grill for two-zone cooking and build a medium-high fire, or heat a gas grill to high. Carefully wipe the preheated grill grates with a lightly oiled paper towel. Using a grill brush, scrape the grill grates clean, then carefully wipe with a lightly oiled towel again.

3. While the grill heats, in a separate bowl, stir together the Cholula, parsley, butter, lemon juice, and garlic.

4. Grill the drumettes over direct heat, flipping and rotating as needed for even cooking, until nicely charred on all sides, 5 to 7 minutes. Move the drumettes to indirect heat, close the grill, and continue to cook, turning the drumettes often (and closing the grill lid in between), until cooked through and the juices run clear (if you're uncertain, cut into one to check), 20 to 25 minutes.

5. Place the hot drumettes in the bowl with the Cholula butter, toss vigorously until well coated, and serve immediately.

WORLDWIDE WINGS

Of course, wings are infinitely flexible, so follow the recipe on page 138, but mix up the sauce to suit your craving or the occasion. Here are a few ideas:

- Swap in FRESH LIME JUICE + CHOPPED FRESH CILANTRO for the lemon juice + parsley

- Use DIJON MUSTARD instead of Cholula + ½ cup (20g) CHOPPED FRESH HERBS (basil, chives, or tarragon)

- Combine 3 to 4 tablespoons PESTO OR OLIVE TAPENADE + 2 tablespoons OLIVE OIL

- Marinate with ½ cup (120ml) TIKI DRESSING (page 99) + CHOPPED FRESH CILANTRO AND MINT + TOASTED SESAME SEEDS

- Use 3 tablespoons PICKLED MUSTARD SEEDS (page 176) + CHOPPED FRESH PARSLEY

- Combine ½ cup (120ml) of your favorite bottled or homemade PEANUT SAUCE + FRESH LIME JUICE + thinly sliced SCALLIONS

Sweet & Smoky Drumsticks

Serves 6 to 8

1 cup (200g) packed dark brown sugar

⅓ cup (80ml) Dijon mustard

Juice of 1 large lemon

1 tablespoon ground coriander

¼ teaspoon cayenne pepper, plus more as desired

2 tablespoons olive oil

Kosher salt and freshly ground black pepper

20 chicken drumsticks

2 cups (180g) wood chips (preferably hickory or oak)

Water or beer (or a combination), for soaking the wood chips

He looks like the famed gypsy guitarist Django Reinhardt, but the real reason I'm smitten with Tim Byres, the chef of Smoke in Dallas (and author of the stellar *Smoke: New Firewood Cooking*), is his devotion to honest, down-home cooking, much of it fired on a grill. These subtly sweet and smoky drumsticks are inspired by one of his recipes. Yes, this method calls for an extended marinade, but the seductive flavors and tender meat are well worth it. Plus, it's easy to whisk together the marinade in the morning and kind of exciting to be ready to roll for a casual weeknight dinner party when you return home. As with wings, it's important to remember that drumsticks require frequent turning to cook evenly and create that beautifully crisp, browned skin that we all want to eat. Twenty drumsticks might seem like a lot, but leftovers make for a very happy lunch (or picnic) the following day.

1. In a bowl, combine the brown sugar, mustard, lemon juice, coriander, cayenne, and olive oil and season with salt and black pepper. Pour the mixture into a large resealable plastic bag. Add the drumsticks and turn to coat. Seal the bag, pressing out the air, and refrigerate for at least 8 or up to 24 hours.

2. About an hour before grilling, remove the drumsticks from the fridge. Soak the wood chips in water for 30 minutes.

3. Prepare a charcoal grill for two-zone cooking and build a medium-high fire, or heat a gas grill to medium-high. Carefully wipe the preheated grill grates with a lightly oiled paper towel. Using a grill brush, scrape the grill grates clean, then carefully wipe with a lightly oiled towel again.

4. Remove the drumsticks from the marinade and season with salt and pepper. Grill the drumsticks over direct heat, turning as needed until all sides are nicely charred, 12 to 15 minutes, then transfer to a baking sheet.

5. Drain the wood chips and scatter them over the coals. If you're using a gas grill, put them in a perforated aluminum foil packet or smoker box and place directly over the flames. When the chips begin to smoke, return the chicken to the grill over indirect heat. Close the grill and smoke the chicken, turning every 5 minutes or so, until an instant-read thermometer inserted into the thickest part of the drumsticks registers 165°F (75°C), 35 to 40 minutes.

6. Transfer the chicken to a serving platter, cover with foil to keep warm, and let rest for 10 minutes before serving.

Chicken Thighs with Rosemary Smoke

Serves 4 to 6

8 bone-in, skin-on
chicken thighs

Olive oil, for drizzling

Kosher salt and freshly
ground black pepper

1 bunch (about 5 big
sprigs) rosemary

A few handfuls arugula

Lemon wedges

When my husband and I spent four years cooking on a ranch in the Texas Hill
Country, where rosemary flourishes (it's "bulletproof," as they say in these
parts), we started using it in just about everything. When the resiny sprigs
are placed on the periphery of hot coals, whatever you're grilling is perfumed
with an intoxicating rosemary smoke. The secret to perfect chicken thighs
is to grill them at a low heat that allows their fat to render and crisp while
the meat gently cooks to juicy perfection. We usually serve these thighs over
arugula with a squeeze of lemon, but they're also delicious with blistered
cherry tomatoes and grilled bread, pasta, or a quinoa pilaf.

1. About an hour before cooking, remove the chicken thighs from the fridge
and place them in a bowl. Drizzle with enough olive oil to lightly coat, season
generously with salt and pepper, and toss to combine.

2. Prepare a charcoal grill for two-zone cooking and build a medium fire, or
heat a gas grill to medium-high. Carefully wipe the preheated grill grates with
a lightly oiled paper towel. Using a grill brush, scrape the grill grates clean,
then carefully wipe with a lightly oiled towel again.

3. When the coals are covered with ash and glowing orangish red with no
black remaining (about 35 minutes after you light the coals), use tongs to lift
the grate and place the rosemary sprigs directly on the periphery of the coals.
Return the grate, then place the thighs on the grill over direct heat and close
the grill. (If you're using a gas grill, put the rosemary in a perforated aluminum
foil packet or in a smoker box.) Cook the thighs, flipping and rotating them
around the heat every 5 minutes or so (closing the grill in between) for even
cooking, about 30 minutes. The chicken skin should be a rich mahogany, and
the meat should feel firm but not dry to the touch. Remove the chicken, cover
with foil, and let rest for 10 minutes.

4. Scatter arugula on a serving platter. Serve the warm or room-temperature
chicken on top, with lemon wedges on the side.

THE SECRET TO SPECTACULAR BONELESS BREASTS

Chicken breasts—particularly the boneless, skinless variety—have gotten a bad rap. Even though they're ubiquitous as an "add-on" protein for salads and such, the lean cut is less than ideal to grill because the breasts can dry out quickly. But they needn't be yawn inducing, because chicken breasts are also the proverbial blank canvas, so you can dress them up to satisfy any craving (which means you have a world of options beyond Caesar salad). And when time is of the essence, there are few things faster to cook on the grill. Here's how to bring out their best by enhancing flavor before and after cooking, as well as some ways to serve them with style.

Before Cooking

With a clean, mild flavor, a chicken breast begs to be seasoned. Start with kosher salt and freshly ground pepper.

Super-lean cuts need added fat for flavor and to prevent them from sticking to the grill. For the best results, coat the meat *and* the preheated cooking grate with oil before cooking.

When time allows (such as the morning before cooking), marinate breasts in a resealable plastic bag with olive oil, salt and pepper, and chopped fresh herbs (thyme, rosemary, oregano, or marjoram are great options) or spice blends (harissa, garam masala, cumin and smoked paprika, or even curry paste moistened with vegetable oil).

The cooking process needs to be quick to avoid drying out the meat, so grill over high heat until the breasts are lightly charred and white throughout, 3 to 4 minutes per side. For faster and more even cooking (hence a lesser chance of overcooking), pound the chicken breasts to an even thickness before grilling.

After Cooking

For the juiciest results, it's essential to let the meat rest for 5 minutes before slicing.

Garnish with big-flavored toppings like olive relish, crumbled aged cheese, salsa, or Green Chile Mayo (page 173).

Give grilled breasts a rich, creamy backdrop by serving them over a slather of hummus (top with hot sauce), feta or goat cheese puree, or Charred Scallion Dressing (page 64).

A FEW FAVORITE COMBINATIONS

Consider each one a ticket to a delicious destination.
These easy-to-assemble and completely crave-worthy
variations deliver every time.

- **BAR PITTI:** Serve pounded, grilled chicken breasts over thinly sliced endive and sun-dried tomatoes. Top with a drizzle of extra-virgin olive oil and flaky salt and serve with a lemon wedge.

- **BANDOL:** Top fresh arugula (or assorted grilled chicories) with chicken and big-flavored ingredients like oil-cured olives and a drizzle of aioli.

- **PERSONAL TRAINER:** Pair chicken breasts with a grain salad, such as one made with farro, freekeh, barley, or quinoa.

- **OTTOLENGHI:** Marinate breasts in harissa-spiked olive oil, then grill and serve sliced in grilled pita bread with cucumber salad and Sumac Yogurt Sauce (page 176).

- **TGV:** Serve chicken breast on a toasted baguette with bánh mì fixings (see Grilled Mushroom Bánh Mì, page 104) or on sourdough bread with crisp bacon, lemony mayo, and sliced tomato.

- **ORTIZ:** Make chicken tacos with a spicy cabbage slaw, sliced avocado, a squeeze of lime, and charred corn tortillas.

Spatchcocked Chicken with Haricots Verts & Grilled Lemons

Serves 2 to 4

One 4- to 4½-pound (1.8 to 2kg) chicken, back and wing tips removed (ask your butcher to spatchcock it for you)

Extra-virgin olive oil, for drizzling

Kosher salt and freshly ground black pepper

1 bunch thyme

8 ounces (225g) haricots verts or green beans, stem ends trimmed

2 spring onions or scallions, halved

2 lemons

Flaky salt

The technique of spatchcocking (butterflying a bird so it lies flat while it cooks) has been around since cooks wore wimples. The method allows more delicious skin to lie flush against the heat so the bird cooks fast and evenly, with crispy, delicious skin. Charred haricots verts and a squeeze of smoky grilled lemon round out a simple and satisfying meal, which you could also serve with Grilled Lemon Mayo (page 81), Salsa Verde (page 176), and a leafy salad.

1. Pat the chicken dry and drizzle both sides with enough olive oil to lightly coat. Generously season with kosher salt and pepper. Spread the thyme sprigs on a baking sheet and lay the seasoned chicken on top, skin side up. Set aside to marinate for 30 minutes at room temperature.

2. Prepare a charcoal grill for two-zone cooking and build a medium-high fire, or heat a gas grill to high. Carefully wipe the preheated grill grates with a lightly oiled paper towel. Using a grill brush, scrape the grill grates clean, then carefully wipe with a lightly oiled towel again. If you're using a gas grill, lower the heat to medium after it preheats to keep the grill around 475°F (245°C).

3. Place the seasoned chicken, skin side down, onto the grill over direct heat and place half of the thyme sprigs on the cavity. Close the grill and cook until the skin is browned, 8 to 10 minutes. Flip the chicken (discarding any burnt sprigs), top with the remaining thyme sprigs, close the grill, and cook until browned and nearly cooked through (an instant-read thermometer inserted into the thickest part of the chicken will read 160°F/70°C), 8 to 10 minutes. Carefully flip once more and cook for 3 to 5 minutes more with the grill uncovered, until the skin is crisp and brown. Transfer the chicken to a rimmed baking sheet to rest.

4. Allow a grill basket to heat for 10 minutes. Place the haricots verts and spring onions in the grill basket and grill over direct heat, stirring often, until lightly charred, about 5 minutes. Meanwhile, cut the lemons in half crosswise, brush the cut side of each lemon with olive oil, and grill over direct heat until browned and slightly charred, 1 to 2 minutes. Transfer to the sheet of grilled chicken. Place the charred haricots verts and onions on a large serving platter and top with the chicken (and any juices that have collected) and the grilled lemons. (You can also slice the grilled onions thinly and mix into the beans.) Drizzle with olive oil, sprinkle with flaky salt, and serve.

Grill-Roasted Chicken with Tomatillo Salsa

Serves 4

One 4- to 4½-pound (1.8 to 2kg) chicken

Kosher salt and freshly ground black pepper

8 to 10 corn tortillas

Taco toppings of your choice (such as thinly sliced cabbage, radishes, and avocado)

Tomatillo Salsa

8 or 9 tomatillos (about 2 pounds/900g), husked and rinsed

1 onion, quartered through the root

2 or 3 serrano or jalapeño chiles (as desired for heat)

2 or 3 cloves garlic, unpeeled

1 cup (20g) fresh cilantro (leaves and tender stems)

1 to 2 tablespoons fresh lime juice

Kosher salt

Warning: The smoky, juicy results of this recipe may prevent you from ever buying rotisserie chicken from the store again. Yes, grilling a whole chicken is a slower game than, say, searing chops, but the delicious payoff will leave you yearning to do it again soon. Depending on the size of your bird, you should plan an hour and change of roasting, but most of that time is unattended (see timeline, page 153). In between, you'll have time to whip together a tomatillo salsa (a fiery condiment you'll enjoy with eggs the next morning—this recipe makes about 4 cups/950ml of it) and prep the rest of the meal (perhaps squeeze a few limes for margaritas).

1. Generously season the chicken with salt and pepper. Position the chicken on a work surface, breast side up, with the legs pointing toward you. Center a 2-foot (60cm) piece of twine under the back of the bird and bring both sides around the wings (securing them to the carcass) and up and around the legs (securing them together). Set aside at room temperature for 30 minutes or up to 1 hour.

2. Meanwhile, make the salsa. Prepare a charcoal grill for two-zone cooking and build a medium fire, or heat a gas grill to medium-high. Carefully wipe the preheated grill grates with a lightly oiled paper towel. Using a grill brush, scrape the grill grates clean, then carefully wipe with a lightly oiled towel again. If you're using a grill basket to make the salsa, allow it to heat for 10 minutes before cooking.

3. Working in batches if necessary, grill the tomatillos, onion, chiles, and garlic (in a grill basket if desired) over direct heat until the vegetables are blackened and blistered on all sides, 4 to 6 minutes for the tomatillos and chiles, a few minutes longer for the onion and garlic. Transfer to a baking sheet to cool.

4. When you're ready to cook the chicken, remove the cooking grate and place a drip pan filled with ½ inch (1.3cm) of water on the side of the grill without coals (if you have a hinged grate, the hinged side should be over the coals).

CONTINUED

Timeline

5:15 p.m. Season chicken

5:20 p.m. Light charcoal chimney

5:35 p.m. Dump hot coals (flames should be rising from chimney)

6:00 p.m. Fire reaches medium heat (350°F to 400°F/175° to 200°C), cook salsa ingredients

6:15 p.m. Salsa ingredients off, chicken on

6:50 p.m. Flip chicken

7:25 p.m. Chicken off (rest 15 to 30 minutes), finish salsa, char tortillas

8:00 p.m. Eat!

5. Return the grate and place the chicken, breast side down, on the grill over the drip pan. (For a gas grill, turn off 1 burner for indirect cooking and place the filled drip pan over the unlit burner). Close the grill and cook, adjusting the vents and gas levels or adding more charcoal as needed to maintain a grill temperature between 350°F and 400°F (175°C and 200°C) for 35 minutes (this is a good time to refill and light your charcoal chimney so you'll have hot coals ready when you need them). Use tongs and a spatula (or your hand if necessary) to carefully flip the chicken breast side up. Close the grill and continue to cook, maintaining the temperature between 350°F and 400°F (175°C and 200°C), until an instant-read thermometer inserted into the thickest part of the thigh registers 165°F (75°C), about 30 minutes more. Toward the end of cooking, move the chicken directly over the heat to brown and crisp the skin, if desired (see below). Let the chicken rest for 15 minutes or up to 30 minutes before carving.

6. While the chicken rests, grill the tortillas over direct heat until lightly charred, about 30 seconds per side. Keep warm in a basket or wrapped in a kitchen towel. Then, finish the salsa. Stem the chiles, peel the garlic, and put them in a food processor. Add the tomatillos, onion, cilantro, and lime juice and process until mostly smooth. Season to taste with salt.

7. Use a knife to quarter or carve the chicken, as desired, and serve with corn tortillas, taco toppings, and tomatillo salsa.

For a Bronzed Bird

Depending on the size of your bird and the temperature of the grill, the chicken might not take on a beautiful browned color over indirect heat. To achieve a darker, crisper skin, move it over direct heat for the last 10 to 20 minutes of cooking, carefully turning and flipping the chicken as needed for even coloring.

Tipsy Chicken with Smoky Pan Drippings

Serves 4

Red Spice Rub

2 tablespoons light brown sugar

2 tablespoons kosher salt

1 tablespoon smoked paprika

1 teaspoon ground coriander

1 teaspoon pure ground chile powder (such as New Mexico)

2 cloves garlic, finely grated

2 tablespoons white wine vinegar

One 12-ounce (355ml) can IPA or citrusy craft brew

One 4- to 4½-pound (1.8 to 2kg) chicken

2 sprigs parsley

2 sprigs oregano

1 lemon, quartered

2 to 3 cups (475 to 710ml) chicken stock or water

Cooked barley or farro

¼ cup (10g) lightly chopped fresh parsley

3 scallions, thinly sliced on the bias

Beer-can chicken is more than just shtick: A beer can provides the base for a whole chicken so it roasts upright, cooking evenly. As the chicken cooks, steam from the beer subtly flavors the meat and keeps it moist. (The setup is less precarious if you use a beer stand, available online, but it's not essential). Plus, any recipe that begins with drinking half a beer is right up my alley. In this recipe, the chicken is slathered with feisty red spices and cooked with a hoppy IPA; it creates a beautifully bronzed bird. Serve this chicken with the outrageously delicious smoky pan drippings and either cooked barley (sticking with the beer theme) or farro.

1. Prepare a charcoal grill for two-zone cooking and build a medium-high fire, or heat a gas grill to high. Carefully wipe the preheated grill grates with a lightly oiled paper towel. Using a grill brush, scrape the grill grates clean, then carefully wipe with a lightly oiled towel again.

2. While the grill heats, make the red spice rub. In a bowl, combine the brown sugar, salt, smoked paprika, coriander, chile powder, garlic, and vinegar and stir until it forms a paste.

3. Drink half the beer. Smile. Season the entire chicken inside and out with the rub and stick the parsley and oregano sprigs and lemon quarters in the cavity. Place the beer can in a metal stand (if using) and then place the cavity of chicken, legs pointing down, onto the open can so that it supports the chicken upright.

4. Remove the cooking grate and place a drip pan filled with ½ inch (1.3cm) of stock on the side of the grill without coals (if you have a hinged grate, the hinged side should be over the coals). For a gas grill, turn off 1 burner for indirect cooking and place the filled drip pan over the unlit burner.

5. Place chicken on the grill above the drip pan over indirect heat. Close the grill and grill the chicken until cooked through and an instant-read thermometer inserted into the thickest part of thigh registers 165°F (75°C), 45 to 60 minutes (refill and light your charcoal chimney right away so you'll have hot coals ready when you need them). To ensure the bird browns evenly, rotate the chicken every 20 minutes. (If using charcoal, you'll probably need to add more after 30 minutes to maintain heat.)

6. Let chicken rest for 15 minutes or up to 30 minutes before carving. Serve with smoky pan drippings (see page 157) and the barley. Garnish with parsley and scallions.

Better Pan Drippings

As the beer-can chicken roasts, its flavorful, smoky juices collect in the drip pan, which is already filled with ½ inch (1.3cm) of stock (or water). Since these juices heat for about an hour, why not make stock? To do this, add the chicken neck you pulled from the bird, a crushed garlic clove, and a few fresh bay leaves to the drip pan before cooking. While the chicken rests, strain the liquid from the drip pan and reduce over medium-high heat in a small saucepan on the stove until it thickens to the desired consistency.

(All Hail) Citrus Ale Chicken

To give the chicken a citrusy flavor, generously season the chicken with kosher salt, freshly ground black pepper, and Szechuan pepper salt. Use a citrusy beer and fill the cavity of the chicken with a couple of swaths of orange and grapefruit peel, 2 fresh bay leaves, and a sprig of oregano.

Hill Country Quail with Greens & Chickpeas

Serves 4

8 partially boned quail

Olive oil, for drizzling

Kosher salt and freshly ground black pepper

1 tablespoon smoked paprika

1 tablespoon pure ground chile powder (such as New Mexico)

1 teaspoon ground cumin

1 teaspoon ground coriander

1 cup (125g) best-quality stone-ground yellow cornmeal

1 bunch mustard greens or lacinato kale, trimmed

2 cloves garlic, crushed

2 or 3 dried arbol chiles

One 15-ounce (425g) can chickpeas, drained

Hot sauce

During our days cooking on a Texas Hill Country ranch, my husband and I learned that autumn and winter mean quail and dove hunts. As a result, the rich, flavorful quail rivals chicken at backyard barbecues here. These days, we spend less time on rural roads, but luckily semi-boneless or partially boned quail is readily available and easy to cook. A quick dredge in cornmeal provides a pebbly texture and crispy crust that enhances the meat and a rub of red spices. A sauté of garlicky greens and chickpeas round out this rustic meal.

1. In a large baking dish, drizzle the quail with enough olive oil to lightly coat and generously season with salt and pepper, using your fingers to carefully rub the seasonings under the skin. In a small bowl, combine the smoked paprika, ground chile, cumin, and coriander. Sprinkle the spices over the birds, using your fingers to rub the spices under the skin, then set aside to marinate.

2. Meanwhile, prepare a charcoal grill for two-zone cooking and build a medium-high fire, or heat a gas grill to high. Carefully wipe the preheated grill grates with a lightly oiled paper towel. Using a grill brush, scrape the grill grates clean, then carefully wipe with a lightly oiled towel again.

3. While the grill heats, place the cornmeal in a shallow dish and lightly season with salt and pepper. Rotate each bird in the spiced oil to ensure they're evenly coated, then dredge in the cornmeal and place on a baking sheet.

4. Grill the quail over direct heat, flipping and rotating as needed for even cooking, until nicely charred on both sides, 4 to 6 minutes on each side. Move the birds to indirect heat, close the grill, and continue to cook, flipping every 3 minutes or so (and closing the grill lid in between), until the coating is golden brown and crisp, the meat is cooked through, and the juices run clear, about 12 minutes. Transfer quail to a rimmed baking sheet.

5. Place a cast-iron skillet on the grill grate over the fire and allow it to heat for 3 to 4 minutes. Tear or chop the greens into pieces. Add a generous drizzle of olive oil to the skillet and then the garlic and chiles. When the garlic sizzles, add the greens, chickpeas, and a sprinkling of salt and cook, tossing with tongs (and closing the grill lid in between tosses), until the greens are wilted, 3 to 4 minutes. Taste for seasoning and add salt or hot sauce, as desired. Serve the warm quail alongside the greens and chickpeas.

Sausage Mixed Grill with Radishes, Beets & Pickled Mustard Seeds

Serves 4

1 cup (240ml) distilled white vinegar, plus more as needed

⅓ cup (65g) sugar

Kosher salt and freshly ground black pepper

1 teaspoon pink peppercorns

1 teaspoon coriander seeds

4 fresh bay leaves

2 dried arbol chiles

12 ounces (340g) mixed young beets—scrubbed, trimmed, and halved lengthwise

8 ounces (225g) mixed radishes, scrubbed, trimmed, and halved

Olive oil, for drizzling

8 fresh or smoked sausages (such as hot or sweet Italian, bratwurst, smoked kielbasa, chorizo, or merguez)

Handful of greens (such as arugula, spinach, or watercress)

½ cup (20g) freshly chopped cilantro

3 tablespoons Pickled Mustard Seeds (page 176)

Grilled bread (see page 21)

Instead of grainy mustard, a grilled link's usual sidekick, these sausages are served alongside a colorful mix of young radishes and beets perked up with pickled mustard seeds. Brining the vegetables before they're grilled infuses them with flavor and preserves moisture. Using a mix of varieties (watermelon, purple daikon, or black radishes; Chioggia and golden beets) creates a stunning plate. Be sure to prick the sausages with a sharp knife before grilling to help them release any excess fat.

1. On the stove top in a saucepan, bring the vinegar, sugar, 2 tablespoons salt, the peppercorns, coriander, bay leaves, chiles, and 3 cups (710ml) water to a boil. Add the beets, lower the heat, and simmer until they're crisp-tender, about 20 minutes. Remove the pan from the heat, add the radishes, and let everything cool in the brine. (You can refrigerate the vegetables in the brine in an airtight container for up to 2 days.)

2. When you're ready to grill, remove the vegetables from the brine, pat them dry, and place them in a large bowl. Discard the brine.

3. Prepare a charcoal grill for two-zone cooking and build a medium-high fire, or heat a gas grill to high. Carefully wipe the preheated grill grates with a lightly oiled paper towel. Using a grill brush, scrape the grill grates clean, then carefully wipe with a lightly oiled towel again.

4. Drizzle the brined vegetables with enough olive oil to lightly coat, season lightly with salt and pepper, and toss to combine. Grill over direct heat, turning occasionally, until lightly charred, 6 to 8 minutes, and then set aside.

5. Grill the sausages over indirect heat, turning and rotating as needed for even cooking, until cooked through, 12 to 15 minutes. In a large bowl, toss together the grilled beets and radishes, greens, cilantro, and mustard seeds. Season with salt and pepper, then taste the vegetables and add more olive oil or vinegar as needed. Serve the vegetables with the sausages and grilled bread.

For a Faster Sausage Grill

If you poach the sausages in water or beer before grilling, they'll require less time on the grates (a few minutes over direct heat should do it).

Porchetta-Style Pork Kebabs with White Beans

Serves 4

8 sturdy rosemary sprigs, ideally about 8 inches (20cm) long

1 pork tenderloin

2 tablespoons freshly chopped thyme leaves

2 cloves garlic, minced

Kosher salt and freshly ground black pepper

Two 15-ounce (425g) cans cannellini beans, drained

3 or 4 fresh bay leaves, torn

Olive oil, for drizzling and brushing

2 large lemons

Traditional Italian porchetta—pork flavored with garlic and herbs—is a showstopper, a massive rolled roast that's a long-cooked affair. It's not gonna happen on a weeknight. But these pretty kebabs made with pork tenderloin and rosemary branches create similar flavors in a fraction of the time. After the meat is charred over high heat, it finishes cooking over white beans that capture the delicious drippings.

1. Remove all the rosemary leaves from the branches except 2 inches (5cm) at the top of each. With a sharp knife, cut the leafless end of each branch at an angle to make a point, which will make it easier to skewer the pork. Coarsely chop the rosemary leaves you removed from the branches.

2. Cut the pork into 1½- to 2-inch (4 to 5cm) pieces and place in a bowl. Season with 2 tablespoons of the chopped rosemary, the thyme, garlic, and a generous sprinkling of salt and pepper. Set aside to marinate at room temperature while you prepare the grill.

3. In an aluminum drip pan, combine the beans, bay leaves, and a generous drizzle of olive oil and season with salt and pepper.

4. Prepare a charcoal grill for two-zone cooking and build a medium-high fire, or heat a gas grill to high. Carefully wipe the preheated grill grates with a lightly oiled paper towel. Using a grill brush, scrape the grill grates clean, then carefully wipe with a lightly oiled towel again.

5. Skewer the pieces of pork with the rosemary sprigs. Avoid packing them too tightly or they won't cook evenly. When you're ready to grill, remove the cooking grate, place the pan of beans alongside the coals, and return the cooking grate. (For a gas grill, turn off 1 burner for indirect cooking and place the filled drip pan over the unlit burner). Brush the pork skewers with olive oil and season with salt and pepper. Grill the pork kebabs over direct heat until nicely browned on each side, 12 to 14 minutes total.

6. Move the kebabs over the drip pan, brush with olive oil again, close the grill, and cook until the pork is cooked through, about 10 minutes. Transfer to a rimmed baking sheet to rest. Remove the beans from the heat, add the zest from 1 lemon, and toss to combine. Halve the lemons crosswise and grill until nicely charred, 1 to 2 minutes. Place beans on serving platter, top with pork skewers and charred lemon halves, and serve.

Porterhouse Pork Chops with Sage-Chile Butter

Serves 4

4 porterhouse (bone-in loin) pork chops, each about 1 inch (2.5cm) thick

Kosher salt and freshly ground black pepper

½ cup (110g) unsalted butter

4 or 5 sprigs sage

2 or 3 dried arbol chiles, as desired for heat

1 clove garlic, crushed

Flaky salt

Few things make me anticipate dinner more than the *hiss* of chops on a hot grill—particularly when they're accompanied by the aroma of an herbaceous butter. Thick and meaty, porterhouse pork chops are more luxurious—and forgiving, thanks to a higher fat content—than other chops. On a charcoal grill, both the meat and the chile-infused herb butter take on an incredible smoky quality. Sage works beautifully with pork, but you can also use rosemary or thyme. Serve these chops alongside crispy grilled potatoes (see page 113), a green vegetable (charred asparagus or any type of pole bean), and grilled bread (see page 21)—and drizzle the butter over everything on the plate.

1. Thoroughly pat the pork chops dry with paper towels. Generously season both sides of the chops with kosher salt and pepper.

2. Prepare a charcoal grill for two-zone cooking and build a medium fire, or heat a gas grill to medium-high. Carefully wipe the preheated grill grates with a lightly oiled paper towel. Using a grill brush, scrape the grill grates clean, then carefully wipe with a lightly oiled towel again.

3. Place the butter, sage, chiles, and garlic in a small cast-iron skillet. Set the skillet over indirect heat until the butter sizzles, a few minutes, and then move the skillet to a cooler corner of the grill or the upper warming rack, if you have one, to keep warm (if you keep the butter in the grill it will continue to absorb the smoky aromas).

4. Grill the chops over direct heat, turning as needed for even cooking, until nicely browned and the internal temperature reaches between 145°F (63°C) for medium-rare and 160°F (70°C) for medium, 15 to 17 minutes. Remove the chops from the grill, cover with aluminum foil, and let rest for 10 minutes.

5. Sprinkle chops with flaky salt and serve with a drizzle of the sage-chile butter.

Bardstown Baby Backs with Bourbon-Mustard Glaze

Serves 4

2 cups (180g) wood chips (preferably hickory, pecan, or oak)

Water or beer (or a combination), for soaking the wood chips

2 racks baby back ribs, about 3 pounds (1.4kg) each

Kosher salt and freshly ground black pepper

½ cup (120ml) Creole mustard (preferably Zatarain's)

½ cup (120ml) cider vinegar

½ cup (120ml) bourbon

3 tablespoons dark brown sugar

It's a revelation to discover you don't need to babysit a low-and-slow fire for hours to have a roll-up-your-sleeves rib feast. Enter baby backs, which are smaller, leaner, and more tender than spareribs, so they can be cooked directly over coals in no more than 30 minutes. I've never been a fan of sweet sauces, but this boozy mustard glaze, inspired by a trip to bourbon country in Kentucky, is right up my alley.

1. Soak the wood chips in water for 30 minutes.

2. About an hour before cooking, season the ribs with salt and pepper and place in a baking dish. Let sit at room temperature while you prepare the grill.

3. Prepare a charcoal grill for two-zone cooking and build a medium fire, or heat a gas grill to medium-high. Carefully wipe the preheated grill grates with a lightly oiled paper towel. Using a grill brush, scrape the grill grates clean, then carefully wipe with a lightly oiled towel again.

4. While the grill heats, on the stove top, combine the mustard, vinegar, bourbon, brown sugar, ½ teaspoon pepper, and pinch of salt in a small saucepan and bring just to a boil over medium heat. Remove from the heat.

5. Drain the wood chips and scatter them over the coals. If using a gas grill, place them in a perforated aluminum foil packet or smoker box directly over the flames.

6. When the chips begin to smoke, grill the ribs over direct heat, flipping and rotating the racks as needed for even cooking until no longer pink, 20 to 25 minutes. Let the meat rest at least 10 minutes, then slice into individual ribs and place them in a large bowl. Pour the bourbon-mustard glaze over the ribs, toss vigorously, and serve.

Beef, Burgers & Lamb

THE BEST BURGERS

Burger enthusiasts are a passionate bunch, with strong and varied opinions about the *ultimate* incarnation. For me, a burger is an indulgence and an occasion, like a steak, so I give them both the same attention to detail (more on steaks later). And I go easy on condiments, so they don't overwhelm the meat—who wants an avalanche of toppings on your plate after you take the first bite?

Start with the best meat.

No matter what variety of meat you're using to make your burger, using freshly ground meat (as opposed to a dense, prepacked block) creates a lighter texture. When it comes to beef, go with an 80/20 percent mix of ground chuck to fat; anything leaner can lead to dry burgers. Use the same approach with other meat varieties. For chicken or turkey burgers, look for ground thigh meat, not breast meat—or consider adding grated zucchini to the mix (a Yotam Ottolenghi trick) for added moisture. For the best flavor, look for pasture-raised or heirloom breeds of meat sourced to specific ranches.

Don't overwork the meat.

For the juiciest results, use a light hand when combining meat varieties and shaping the patties—overmixing will create a tough, dense burger.

Shape it right.

I learned a couple of invaluable tricks from J. Kenji López-Alt's burger explorations for his book *The Food Lab*. He points out that burgers shrink during cooking, so to avoid the mismatch of a small patty lost in a giant bun, you should make sure the diameter of the uncooked patty is ½ inch (1.3cm) larger than the bun. Then use your thumb to create a small indentation in the center of patty, which prevents the meat from contracting and bulging up in middle. That means they stay hefty, because if you don't need two hands to hold a burger, you've done something wrong.

Only season the exterior.

Working salt and pepper into the meat when you're shaping the patties results in a dense, springy texture, because the salt begins to dissolve proteins in the meat, causing them to cross-link with each other. Get around this by seasoning only the outside of your patty, but doing so generously (another tip from Kenji).

Flip frequently.

Relying on a single flip allows the upward-facing side to lose too much heat. Frequent flipping (and moving the burger to the cooler part of the two-zone fire, as needed, to avoid flare-ups) cooks both sides simultaneously and helps the meat cook more evenly. Whatever you do, resist the urge to press the burger with your spatula, as this squeezes out flavorful juices.

Let it rest.

Yes, it's difficult not to dig right in to a hot, juicy burger. But, as with other meats, allowing the patty to rest for a few minutes allows the hot juices to settle and results in a more satisfying flavor and texture.

Green Chile Cheeseburgers

Serves 4

1 pound (450g) freshly ground beef chuck (80/20 mix)

1 pound (450g) freshly ground pork

Kosher salt and freshly ground black pepper

4 slices Monterey Jack or sharp cheddar cheese

4 burger buns, split

Pickled Red Onions (optional; page 176)

Leaf lettuce (optional)

Green Chile Mayo

4 Hatch chiles (or a mix of poblano, cubanelle, and Anaheim chiles)

2 serrano chiles

1 cup (220g) mayonnaise (preferably Duke's)

3 tablespoons freshly chopped cilantro (leaves and tender stems)

1 tablespoon fresh lime juice, plus more as desired

Kosher salt and freshly ground black pepper

Every August, markets throughout Texas celebrate the arrival of Hatch chiles from New Mexico with festivals and heaps of fragrant, fire-roasted chiles. Because I pine for their smoky, herbal heat all year long, I char Hatch and other varieties—poblano, Anaheim, cubanelle—on the grill to make salsa verde, pozole, and the smoky mayo spread you see here. Heat levels vary from pepper to pepper (even within the same variety), so taste them after roasting and adjust the amount you use accordingly. A mix of beef and pork creates a juicy, flavorful burger that's particularly delicious with this spicy mayo and the tart-sweet crunch of pickled red onions.

1. In a large bowl, gently combine the beef and pork, being careful not to overwork the meat. Divide into 4 portions. Press each portion into a patty that's about ½ inch (1.3cm) wider on all sides than your burger buns, pressing gently until they hold together. Form a slight dimple in the center of each patty. Season the top and bottom sides liberally with salt and pepper. Refrigerate if not using right away.

2. Prepare a charcoal grill for two-zone cooking and build a medium-high fire, or heat a gas grill to high. Carefully wipe the preheated grill grates with a lightly oiled paper towel. Using a grill brush, scrape the grill grates clean, then carefully wipe with a lightly oiled towel again. If you're using a grill basket, allow it to heat for 10 minutes before cooking.

3. To make the green chile mayo, place the chiles perpendicular to the grates (or in a preheated grill basket) and grill over direct heat, turning and rotating as needed for even cooking, until charred on all sides, 3 to 4 minutes. Transfer to a bowl, cover with a kitchen towel (this will make their skins easier to remove), and let rest for about 10 minutes. Using your hands or a paring knife, gently remove the charred skins from the chiles, then seed and chop them. In another bowl, stir together the chiles with the mayo, cilantro, and lime juice, and then season with salt and pepper. Set aside or refrigerate for up to 1 day.

4. Grill the burgers over direct heat, flipping and rotating as needed for even cooking (move patties away from direct heat if flare-ups occur), until they register 125°F (52°C) for medium-rare or 135°F (57°C) for medium, 10 to 12 minutes. Top the burgers with cheese slices during the last minute of cooking. Let rest on a large plate for 3 to 5 minutes. Meanwhile, toast the buns over direct heat. Spread the bottom bun with the green chile mayo and top with the burger, the pickled red onions, and lettuce. Serve immediately.

Straight-Up Lamb Burgers

Serves 4

2 pounds (900g) freshly ground lamb

Kosher salt and freshly ground black pepper

½ cup (110g) mayonnaise (preferably Duke's)

3 tablespoons Creole mustard (preferably Zatarain's)

4 burger buns, split

4 thin slices feta cheese

Thin slices of red onion

The problem with most lamb burgers is that they're packed with too many ingredients that are meant to *convince* you to order the lamb burger: herbs, spices, cheese, olives. Where's the lamb? That sort of fanfare always feels suspicious. When I crave lamb, I want to taste its entirely unique character, a wild flavor that always evokes the herbaceous, sun-scorched terrain of the Texas Hill Country for me. When it comes to condiments, I keep it simple with a thin slice of feta, sliced onions, and a slather of mayo spiked with zippy Creole mustard. If you want to mix up the mayo even more, add finely chopped rosemary, garlic, or lemon zest to the spread.

1. Divide the lamb into 4 portions. Press each portion into a patty that's about ½ inch (1.3cm) wider on all sides than your burger buns, pressing gently until they hold together, but taking care not to overwork them. Form a slight dimple in the center of each patty. Season the top and bottom sides with salt and pepper. Refrigerate if not using right away.

2. Combine the mayonnaise and mustard in a bowl.

3. Prepare a charcoal grill for two-zone cooking and build a medium-high fire, or heat a gas grill to high. Carefully wipe the preheated grill grates with a lightly oiled paper towel. Using a grill brush, scrape the grill grates clean, then carefully wipe with a lightly oiled towel again.

4. Grill the burgers over direct heat, flipping and rotating as needed for even cooking (move patties away from the fire if flare-ups occur), until they register 125°F (52°C) for medium-rare or 135°F (57°C) for medium, 10 to 12 minutes. Let rest on a large plate for 2 to 3 minutes. Meanwhile, toast the buns over direct heat. Spread the bottom bun with the mayo-mustard mixture and top with the burger followed by a slice of feta and onion. Serve immediately.

Delicious Sidekicks for Grilled Meat

The bright pop of pickled vegetables, vibrant green sauce, and spiced, creamy yogurt take any grilled meat to the next level.

Pickled Red Onions

Add 2 thinly sliced red onions to a pot of boiling water and cook for 1 minute, then drain. Return the onions to the pan with 1½ cups (355ml) red wine vinegar or cider vinegar, 2 fresh bay leaves, 1 tablespoon sugar, 1 tablespoon salt, 1 teaspoon coriander seeds, and enough water to barely cover the onions. Bring to a boil over high heat, simmer 1 minute, and then pour the mixture into a glass jar to cool. Refrigerate for at least 2 hours, until the mixture is cold. Onions will crisp as they cool and keep for several weeks in the fridge. *Good with Green Chile Cheeseburgers (page 173) and Skirt Steak Tacos (page 189).*

Pickled Mustard Seeds

Rinse ¾ cup (140g) yellow mustard seeds in a fine-mesh sieve, pat dry with paper towels, and place in an 8-ounce (240ml) glass jar or heatproof bowl. In a small heavy saucepan, combine 1 cup (240ml) distilled white vinegar, ⅓ cup (65g) sugar, 3 or 4 dried piquín chiles or 1 dried arbol chile, and ½ teaspoon kosher salt. Bring the mixture to a boil over medium heat, stirring to dissolve the sugar. Pour the hot liquid over the mustard seeds and let them soak at room temperature until softened, 3 to 4 hours. Store pickled mustard seeds in a sealed jar or container in the fridge for up to 1 month. *Good with Broccoli Spears with Crispy Cheese Crust (page 57), wings (see page 138), and sausages (see page 161).*

Salsa Verde

In a food processor, combine 1 crushed garlic clove, 2 anchovies, 1 tablespoon capers, 2 teaspoons Dijon mustard, a pinch of red pepper flakes, and ½ teaspoon kosher salt and pulse until the mixture is coarsely chopped. Add 1 cup (20g) fresh parsley leaves, ½ cup (10g) fresh mint leaves, and ½ cup (10g) fresh basil and process until combined, then slowly drizzle in ½ cup (120ml) olive oil (or more as needed for the desired texture). Add the finely grated zest of 1 lemon and fresh lemon juice to taste and season with salt and freshly ground pepper. Store in a sealed container in the fridge for 3 to 4 days. *Good with Basic Grilled Fish (page 112), Spatchcocked Chicken with Haricots Verts & Grilled Lemons (page 148), and Skirt Steak (page 189).*

Sumac Yogurt Sauce

In a small bowl, stir together 1¼ cups (300ml) Greek yogurt with 3 tablespoons extra-virgin olive oil, 2 tablespoons fresh lemon juice, 2 teaspoons sumac, 1 teaspoon finely grated lemon zest, 1 minced garlic clove, and a pinch of cayenne until smooth. Feel free to omit the sumac, or use ground cumin, coriander, or harissa instead. You can also add freshly chopped parsley or mint. Store in a sealed container in the fridge for 3 to 4 days. *Good with Basic Grilled Fish (page 112), crispy rounds of grilled potatoes (see page 113), chicken breasts (see page 146), and Boneless Leg of Lamb (page 182).*

Hot Dog Night

Makes 8 hot dogs

8 all-beef hot dogs
(preferably uncured
organic or grass-fed)

8 hot dog buns, split

Condiments of choice
(see page 180 for ideas)

For most of us, biting into a hot dog—the snap of crisp skin, juicy meat, spicy mustard—is an iconic summer pleasure. But grilling hot dogs at home is a no-brainer any night—they need only a few moments over medium-high heat, and the confluence of interesting condiments and other tasty components (toasted bun, cold beer) add up to a spectacular experience; see some suggestions for condiments and combos on the pages that follow.

Start with the best-quality all-beef franks you can find. For me, that means organic, uncured, or grass-fed varieties from Certified Humane producers. It's important to cook over moderate heat and keep your tongs in hand so you can keep those dogs moving. Cooking at too high a heat will result in split or scorched dogs.

1. Prepare a charcoal grill for two-zone cooking and build a medium-high fire, or heat a gas grill to high. Carefully wipe the preheated grill grates with a lightly oiled paper towel. Using a grill brush, scrape the grill grates clean, then carefully wipe with a lightly oiled towel again.

2. Grill the hot dogs over direct heat until charred and heated through (they'll turn a shade darker and look taut), 3 to 4 minutes. Set aside to rest while you toast the buns.

3. Serve immediately with your favorite condiments.

The Secret to Plumper Dogs

To help prevent hot dogs from shriveling (and to create a delicious crispy texture, to boot), slice an X into each end. When the dogs hit the grill, these slits expand and allow the heat to permeate the meat more quickly, resulting in a shorter cooking time and a plumper, juicier dog. This is particularly helpful with higher-fat franks and fresh sausages (leaner dogs from grass-fed beef, for instance, need less cooking time and won't plump as much).

Killer Condiments

Celery Root Remoulade

In a bowl, whisk together ½ cup (110g) mayonnaise, 3 tablespoons sour cream or crème fraîche, 2 tablespoons olive oil, 2 tablespoons fresh lemon juice, 1 heaping tablespoon Dijon mustard, 1 teaspoon poppy seeds (or ½ teaspoon celery seeds), and 1 teaspoon kosher salt. Using a food processor, grate 1 peeled large celery root (you should have about 3 cups/270g) and combine with the dressing, tossing well to evenly coat. Taste for seasoning and add more lemon juice, salt, and pepper as desired. Refrigerate for up to 3 days.

Easy Cornichon Relish

In a food processor, combine 2 cups (460g) chopped cornichons (including any small pickled onions that might be in the jar), 1 cup (240g) chopped kosher dill pickles, 1 chopped shallot, 2 tablespoons tarragon vinegar, 1 tablespoon Dijon mustard, and 1 teaspoon chopped fresh thyme and process until coarsely chopped. Transfer to an airtight container and refrigerate for up to 3 weeks.

Gingery Beet Ketchup

In a saucepan over high heat, bring to a boil 1 cup (240ml) cider vinegar, ¼ cup (40g) diced red onion, ¼ cup packed (50g) light brown sugar, 3 tablespoons grated fresh ginger, and 1 pound (450g) cooked, peeled, and diced red beets. Lower the heat and simmer until thickened and the vegetables are very tender, about 12 minutes. Remove beets from the heat, cool slightly, and then puree in a food processor with 1 teaspoon kosher salt, ½ teaspoon ground coriander, a pinch of ground allspice, and freshly ground pepper to taste until very smooth (add water if needed for desired consistency). Transfer to an airtight container and refrigerate for up to 2 weeks. Makes about 3 cups (710ml). Also great with grilled cheese!

Pickled Banana Peppers

Stem and thinly slice 8 ounces (225g) fresh hot yellow banana (or Hungarian wax) peppers. In a small saucepan, combine 1 cup (240ml) distilled white vinegar, ¾ cup (175ml) water, ¼ cup (50g) sugar, 1½ teaspoons kosher salt, and 1 teaspoon yellow mustard seeds and bring to a boil over high heat, stirring to dissolve sugar. Remove from the heat and add the sliced peppers, pressing gently to submerge them in liquid. Let cool. Transfer the peppers to a glass jar, add just enough brine to cover, and refrigerate until cold and crisp (they'll last up to 2 months). Feel free to pickle an equal amount of carrot batons, sliced radishes, young turnips, or green beans in this brine.

Shiner Bock Kraut

Melt 2 tablespoons unsalted butter in a skillet over medium-high heat, add 1 sliced large sweet onion, a pinch each of kosher salt and freshly ground pepper, and sauté until the onion is tender, 6 to 8 minutes. Add 2 tablespoons light brown sugar, 2 tablespoons Creole mustard, a pinch of caraway seeds, 1 cup (240ml) Shiner Bock (or other amber beer), and 1 pound (450g) store-bought refrigerated sauerkraut (rinsed and drained) and simmer, stirring, until the liquid has reduced by half, about 8 minutes. Season with salt and pepper and serve warm, or refrigerate for up to 1 week.

DRESSING YOUR DOG

A squirt of yellow mustard will suffice, but here are
a few other enticing ways to gussy up your dog.

- THE BETH ANN Gingery Beet Ketchup (opposite) +
  Pickled Banana Peppers (opposite) + feta

- EL RODEO Saucy charro beans + a drizzle of queso
  (the melted kind made with Velveeta and Ro-tel chiles) +
  sliced scallions

- FRANK-O-PHILE Celery Root Remoulade (opposite) +
  shaved breakfast radishes + chervil

- FRENCH PICNIC Easy Cornichon Relish (opposite) +
  mayo + shredded carrots

- MUCHO MACHITO Bacon-wrapped dogs (you'll need
  to cook them slowly, over indirect heat, until the bacon
  crisps) + grated cheddar (or slices of American cheese) +
  pickled jalapeños

- RED ROOSTER Kimchi + thinly sliced cabbage + sriracha
  mayo + chopped roasted salted peanuts

- TOO FAT POLKA Shiner Bock Kraut (opposite) +
  potato salad + thinly sliced jalapeños

Boneless Leg of Lamb with Sumac Yogurt Sauce

Serves 6 to 8

One 4- to 5-pound
(1.8 to 2.3kg) boneless
leg of lamb, butterflied

Olive oil, for drizzling

Kosher salt and freshly
ground black pepper

2 tablespoons freshly
chopped rosemary

2 tablespoons freshly
chopped oregano

1 tablespoon ground
cumin

1 tablespoon ground
coriander

2 or 3 cloves garlic,
crushed

Sumac Yogurt Sauce
(page 176)

Perfumed with Mediterranean flavors and charred over a hot fire, a boneless leg of lamb makes an impressive and surprisingly easy meal to prepare on the grill. The major perk of grilling a boneless leg is that more of the meat comes in direct contact with the grates, so you end up with more crisp, browned, delicious crust. Serve the sliced meat and its juices with olives, a simple cucumber salad, Sumac Yogurt Sauce, grilled slices of young eggplant or zucchini, and grilled pita.

1. Drizzle the lamb with enough olive oil to lightly coat on all sides and generously season with salt and pepper, using your hands to evenly coat the meat. Combine the rosemary, oregano, cumin, coriander, and garlic in a small bowl and rub the mixture evenly all over the lamb. Set aside to marinate at room temperature for 1 hour.

2. Prepare a charcoal grill for two-zone cooking and build a medium-high fire, or heat a gas grill to high. Carefully wipe the preheated grill grates with a lightly oiled paper towel. Using a grill brush, scrape the grill grates clean, then carefully wipe with a lightly oiled towel again.

3. Grill the lamb skin side down over direct heat, flipping and rotating as needed for even cooking, until well browned with grill marks on all sides and the meat registers 125°F to 130°F (52°C to 55°C) for medium-rare. Depending on the size and shape of the lamb leg, cooking times will vary anywhere from 8 to 10 minutes for smaller pieces and up to 20 minutes for larger sections. Transfer the lamb to a carving board and let it rest for at least 10 minutes. Thinly slice against the grain and serve with yogurt sauce.

Cowgirl Strip Steaks with Pink Peppercorn Crust

Serves 4

Pink Peppercorn Crust

3 tablespoons pink peppercorns, plus more for garnish

1 tablespoon Szechuan peppercorns

1 tablespoon coriander seeds

1 teaspoon fennel seeds

1 tablespoon plus 1 teaspoon kosher salt

½ teaspoon dried orange peel

½ teaspoon cayenne or another ground red chile

Four 8- to 10-ounce (225 to 285g) boneless New York strip steaks

2 small heads frisée, torn into bite-size pieces, or a few handfuls of peppery greens (such as watercress, arugula, or mizuna)

Flaky salt

1 lemon, quartered

I developed this fragrant spice blend when my husband and I were cooking on a ranch (a version of this recipe ran in my first cookbook, *Cowgirl Cuisine*), and I've been using it to season steaks ever since. I love how the subtle heat of the peppercorns perfumes the rich, meaty flavor of strip steaks. Grilling a great steak isn't complicated, but attention to a few key details will up your game.

The first and arguably most important step is to season the meat—generously—an hour in advance (as in, well before you fire up the grill). This allows the seasonings to permeate the cut for a fuller flavor and the meat to come to room temperature, so it cooks evenly. It's also important to build a two-zone fire, so you have some flexibility with the heat. You might need to move the meat (or briefly close the grill) to avoid flare-ups or to finish cooking the meat through without burning the crust.

You definitely don't want to overcook the beautiful piece of meat you've splurged on, so don't forget to account for carryover cooking, which means taking the steak off the heat just *before* it reaches your desired doneness (if you think you waited too long, see the tip at the end of the recipe). Finally, let the steak rest for 10 minutes to allow the cut to reabsorb all of its flavorful juices; this also gives you time to grill bread for soaking up the delicious juices and pop open a bottle of your best red.

My favorite way to serve this steak is alongside (or over) a simple salad of feathery frisée. The bitter greens are the perfect foil for the meat's richness, and the juices from the steak provide the "dressing"; add an additional drizzle of olive oil or a squeeze of lemon, if you'd like. If you want further embellishment, add sliced avocado, oil-cured olives, crumbled blue cheese or chèvre, or grilled bread crumbs (see page 21) to the mix.

1. To make the pink peppercorn crust, heat the peppercorns, coriander, and fennel seeds in a small, dry skillet over medium heat, shaking the seeds occasionally, until fragrant and lightly toasted, 2 to 3 minutes. Let cool and transfer to a mortar. Add the kosher salt, orange peel, and cayenne and coarsely grind with the pestle; you can also combine them in a resealable plastic bag and roll a wine bottle over.

2. About an hour before grilling, remove the steaks from the fridge and coat all sides with the spice mix. Marinate at room temperature for 1 hour.

3. Meanwhile, prepare a charcoal grill for two-zone cooking and build a medium-high fire, or heat a gas grill to high. Carefully wipe the preheated grill grates with a lightly oiled paper towel. Using a grill brush, scrape the grill grates clean, then carefully wipe with a lightly oiled towel again.

4 Grill the steaks over direct heat until charred and crusty on both sides and the meat registers 120°F (49°C) for rare, 4 to 5 minute per side. Carryover cooking will bring the steak to 125°F (52°C), or medium-rare, as it rests. Transfer to a carving board.

5 Cut each steak into ½-inch (1.3cm) slices. Place the frisée on a platter and arrange the steak slices on top, drizzling the juices over the frisée. Sprinkle with flaky salt and serve with lemon wedges.

Meat Under- or Overcooked? Rest It Right

One night over palomas and grilled octopus, Andrew Curren, the talented chef (and my husband's partner) at Easy Tiger and Italic in Austin, taught me an invaluable lesson in how to control carryover cooking. The way you lay out hot grilled steaks to rest, he explained, makes a difference in the duration of their carryover heat from the grill. Placing the hot side of the steak down (the last side to touch the grates) retains more heat, whereas placing the hotter side up allows the heat to diffuse more quickly. So, if you're worried that a steak is slightly overcooked, let it rest hot side up. If you're worried the meat is undercooked, rest it hot side down.

Skirt Steak with Salsa Verde

Serve 4

One 2½-pound (1.1kg)
skirt steak, cut into 4 to
6 pieces

Olive oil, for drizzling

Kosher salt and freshly
ground black pepper

Salsa Verde (page 176)

Skirt steak is a meat lover's cut—and the favorite of many chefs. That's because of the three "flat steaks" (along with flank and hanger), skirt has the most fat, so it's juicier and meatier. The trick to enhancing tenderness is to give the skirt a quick, strong sear on both sides before the inside overcooks. After the meat rests, slice it thinly against the grain (this cuts through the muscle fibers, and shorter fibers are less tough). Remember that meat will continue to cook after it's taken off the heat, so pull it when it's slightly *less* done than you like it. With its pop of herbaceous flavor, Italian salsa verde brightens any grilled meat or fish.

1. About an hour before grilling, remove the steak from the fridge. Drizzle with enough olive oil to lightly coat on both sides and generously season with salt and pepper. Set aside to marinate at room temperature for 1 hour.

2. Meanwhile, prepare a charcoal grill for two zone cooking and build a medium-high grill, or light a gas grill to high. Carefully wipe the preheated grill grates with a lightly oiled paper towel. Using a grill brush, scrape the grates clean, then carefully wipe with a lightly oiled towel again.

3. Place the steak fat side down over direct heat. If the coals flare up, close the lid for a few seconds to snuff out the fire. After a few minutes, rotate the steaks 90 degrees (keeping the fat side down) to expose different surfaces to the ambient heat. When the bottom is nicely charred, 6 to 8 minutes, flip the steaks and cook until the meat registers 120°F (49°C) for rare or 125°F (52°C) for medium-rare, 4 to 6 minutes. Transfer to a carving board and let rest for 5 minutes. Thinly slice against the grain and serve with the salsa verde (and a Diego's Paloma, page 17).

Skirt Steak Tacos with Red Chile Rub

If you'd rather grill skirt steak for tacos, in a small bowl, combine 1 tablespoon ground cumin, 1 tablespoon smoked paprika, 1 tablespoon pure ground chile powder (such as New Mexico), and 2 cloves minced garlic and add enough olive oil to make a rich paste. Season the steaks with kosher salt and freshly ground pepper, then evenly rub the spice paste over the meat. Set aside to marinate at room temperature for 30 minutes or up to 1 hour. Cook as directed. Serve the sliced meat in flour or corn tortillas with guacamole, Pickled Red Onions (page 176) or chopped onions, and chopped fresh cilantro with a squeeze of lime.

Charred Steak Tips with Asian Herb Salad

Serves 4 to 6

2 pounds (900g) sirloin
steak tips (cut from
flap steak)

Olive oil, for drizzling

Kosher salt and freshly
ground black pepper

Asian Herb Salad
¼ cup (60ml) fish sauce
(preferably Red Boat)

¼ cup (60ml) fresh
lime juice

2 tablespoons minced
fresh ginger

2 tablespoons minced
fresh lemongrass, using
inner core from bottom
third of stalk

1 tablespoon toasted
sesame oil

1 tablespoon dark
brown sugar

1 or 2 red or green
Thai or serrano chiles,
stemmed and thinly
sliced

1 cup (20g) fresh Thai
basil leaves, torn or
coarsely chopped

½ cup (10g) coarsely
chopped fresh cilantro
(leaves and tender stems)

½ cup (10g) coarsely
chopped fresh mint
leaves

4 scallions, thinly sliced
on the bias

When I'm craving the brightness and heat of Asian flavors—lime, lemongrass, ginger, chiles—and the meaty satisfaction of charred beef, this is my kind of meal. Steak tips are inexpensive and full of flavor—most butchers will have them for you, but you can also make them yourself by cutting flap steak (also called bavette or sirloin tip) into 2-inch (5cm) chunks. And because they're a thinner cut, they cook quickly, making this an easy and way-better-than-takeout meal to knock out after a long day. You can serve the meat atop a tangle of rice or soba noodles or steamed jasmine rice, on a toasted baguette for a killer sandwich, or over a tumble of leaf lettuces.

1. Prepare a charcoal grill for two-zone cooking and build a medium-high fire, or heat a gas grill to high. Carefully wipe the preheated grill grates with a lightly oiled paper towel. Using a grill brush, scrape the grill grates clean, then carefully wipe with a lightly oiled towel again.

2. Drizzle the steak tips with enough olive oil to lightly coat, then lightly season with salt and pepper and toss to combine.

3. While the grill preheats, start the salad. In a large bowl, whisk together the fish sauce, lime juice, ginger, lemongrass, sesame oil, brown sugar, and chiles. Set it aside while you cook the meat; the sugar will continue to dissolve.

4. Grill the steak tips over direct heat, flipping and rotating frequently so they get deeply browned on all sides, 7 to 9 minutes for medium-rare. To check doneness, use a sharp knife to slice into 1 of the chunks. Remember that you want the meat cooked a bit less than you like because it will continue to cook after it's taken off the heat. Place the warm meat in the bowl with the dressing. Add the Thai basil, cilantro, mint, and scallions and toss vigorously to coat. Let the meat rest 5 minutes before serving.

For a Crisper Steak Crust

———

To preserve a steak's crisp crust, let it rest on a wire rack set above a rimmed baking sheet.

Rebel Tomahawk

Serves 4 (or 8, if you're not in Texas)

Two 2-pound (900g) tomahawk steaks, 1½ to 2 inches (4 to 5cm) thick

Kosher salt and freshly cracked black pepper

Flaky salt

When I'm in need of a meat whisperer, I call my friend Aaron Franklin, the brilliant pitmaster at Franklin Barbecue in Austin. As a guy who spends endless hours over staggering quantities of meat and wood fires, he has plenty of hard-won expertise and lots of good advice. So before I grilled my first tomahawk, a massive and expensive rib eye distinguished by its long bone, I called him up.

According to Aaron, the challenge in grilling such a big honking piece of meat is cooking it through without burning the exterior. To achieve those results, Aaron flips the usual formula for grilling steaks. Instead of searing the meat over a hot fire, he relies on a "reverse sear" in which the steaks are grilled slowly over medium-low heat, then finished directly on a bed of hot, glowing coals (you can use the technique for just about any substantial, well-marbled cuts, like tri-tip or filet). It's a great method for entertaining because you can cook the meat in advance, hang out with friends, and then finish the steaks on the grill (dinner theater!) just before serving. This steak is delicious with classic accompaniments like Caesar salad and grilled corn (see page 93), with charred shishito peppers on the side.

1. About an hour before cooking, generously season the steaks with kosher salt and pepper, rubbing with your hands to form an even crust. Prepare a charcoal grill for two-zone cooking and build a low (250°F/120°C) fire.

2. Grill the steak over direct heat, flipping every few minutes for even cooking, until it registers between 110°F and 115°F (43°C and 46°C), about 45 minutes.

3. Remove the steak and rest it until you're ready to finish the meat, at least 30 minutes or up to 3 hours. In the meantime, start another chimney of charcoal to create a very high heat for searing.

4. To finish, place the steak directly on the glowing embers and cook until a nice, dark crust forms and the steak reaches 135°F (57°C), about 5 minutes per side. Use 2 sets of tongs to remove the steak from the coals—use 1 pair to grab the steak up by its bone and another pair to tap off any coals or ash.

5. Let the meat rest for 10 minutes, then slice against the grain into ¼- to ½-inch (6mm to 1.3cm) slices, pour the juices over the meat, sprinkle with flaky salt, and serve.

THE SMOKY-SWEET CHARM
OF GRILLED DESSERTS

———

Grilled desserts don't really require a recipe—they just call for a bit of resourcefulness. Like an oven, the heat of a grill can toast and deepen the flavor of day-old bread and baked goods and caramelize natural sugars in fruit. And perhaps best of all, grilled desserts are easy to assemble, so when it comes to dessert, why not make the most of the fire that cooked your dinner to lend a smoky sweetness to whatever you have on hand? Follow this formula as a general guide:

START WITH A GRILLED BASE: Breads, baked items, or fruit.

GRILL FRUIT: Heat a grill to medium-high heat. Slice the fruit as desired for presentation, being mindful of its density and how it will hold up on the grill. For instance, juicy plums, peaches, figs, and apricots will soften quickly; I halve them so they hold together and they're easier to remove from the grill. Slice firmer fruits that benefit from a sear on two sides, like pineapple or star fruit, into slices or long spears. In general, lean toward larger pieces—small, bite-size chunks tend to break down. In a bowl, toss fruit with enough olive oil to lightly coat (or brush the fruit slices to coat if you're worried about them breaking down). Grill until charred in spots (anywhere from 3 to 8 minutes). To limit the amount of crumble between the grates or your luscious peach tasting like the steak you just grilled, use an oiled and preheated grill basket set over direct heat (or even a grill pan) to grill your dessert components.

ADD SOMETHING CREAMY & SWEET: Ice cream, crème fraîche, whipped cream, and so on, and/or a spoonful of something sweet and/or acidic (jam or a honeyed vinegar).

FINISH WITH A CRUNCHY TOPPING: Mix and match from the ideas opposite to find your favorite combinations, and see some of mine on page 198.

BAKED ITEMS	GRILLED FRUIT	CREAMY	SWEET & ACIDIC	CRUNCHY TOPPINGS
Grilled bread (sourdough, whole grain, levain, or enriched white breads like brioche or *pain de mie*)	Figs	Nutella	Marmalade	Granola
	Mango	Nut butters	Jam	Cacao nibs
	Pineapple	Flavored butters	Honey	Toasted nuts
Pound cake	Star fruit	Fresh cheese (fromage blanc, quark)	Maple syrup	Toasted seeds (sesame, pumpkin, sunflower)
Quick breads (banana, poppy seed, pumpkin)	Stone fruit (plums, apricots, peaches, nectarines)	Cream cheese	Sorghum	Crumbled pralines or toffee
Buttermilk biscuits	Bananas	Lemon or lime curd		Crushed cookies (gingersnaps, oatmeal, peanut butter sandwich cookies)
Day-old muffins or bar cookies	Citrus fruit	Crème fraîche		Grilled bread crumbs (see page 21)
		Toasted marshmallows		
		Salted caramel sauce		
		Bittersweet chocolate sauce		

MAKE YOUR FAVORITES

A FEW FAVORITE COMBINATIONS

Luscious grilled desserts usually begin with whatever's on hand (gingersnaps?) and then follow the whim of a current craving (salted caramel!). However, the confluence of certain textures and flavors (like the ones that follow) are hard to beat.

- THIN SLICES OF GRILLED RYE + BITTERSWEET CHOCOLATE (shaved for quick melting) + FLAKY SALT

- GRILLED CHOCOLATE QUICK BREAD + CRÈME FRAÎCHE + RASPBERRIES

- GRILLED POUND CAKE (citrus or vanilla) + GRILLED PEACHES + GINGER OR VANILLA ICE CREAM

- GRILLED BUTTERMILK BISCUITS + SLICED STRAWBERRIES + MARSHMALLOW CREAM + DARK CHOCOLATE SHAVINGS

- GRILLED FIGS + COFFEE ICE CREAM + BOURBON

- GRILLED PINEAPPLE SLICES (brushed with rum and vanilla bean paste) + PASSION FRUIT SORBET

- GRILLED MANGO HALVES (grill cut side down, then slice into strips or cubes) + GRILLED LIME JUICE + COCONUT GELATO

- GRILLED BANANAS + CHOCOLATE ICE CREAM + CRÈME DE CACAO + WHISKEY

ANATOMY OF A S'MORE

As an enthusiastic camper and mother of two scouts, I'm frequently reminded that the classic s'more (graham crackers, toasted marshmallows, Hershey's chocolate bar) has stood the test of time for a reason—it's perfect. In fact, it might seem that meddling with the equation is unnecessary or just plain wrong, like remaking an Elvis hit. And yet, spectacular things can come from tweaking tradition (have you heard Lucinda Williams's version of Gram Parsons's "Return of the Grievous Angel"?). All you need is a sandwich base that stands in for the graham cracker, something gooey and creamy to meld the goodness together, and anything else you might crave. Here, a flurry of options:

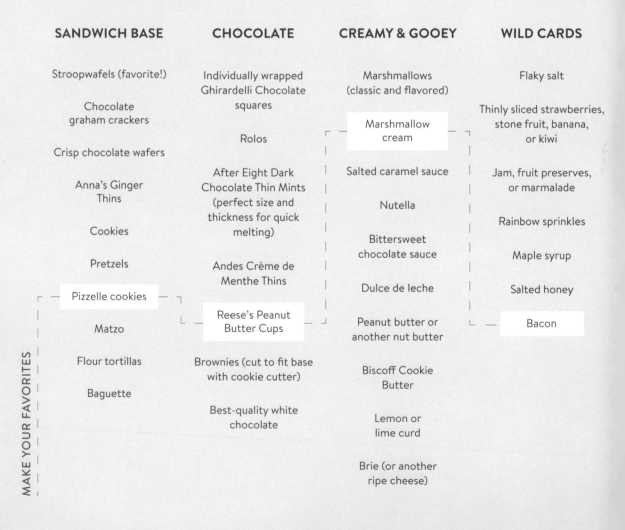

SANDWICH BASE	CHOCOLATE	CREAMY & GOOEY	WILD CARDS
Stroopwafels (favorite!)	Individually wrapped Ghirardelli Chocolate squares	Marshmallows (classic and flavored)	Flaky salt
Chocolate graham crackers	Rolos	Marshmallow cream	Thinly sliced strawberries, stone fruit, banana, or kiwi
Crisp chocolate wafers	After Eight Dark Chocolate Thin Mints (perfect size and thickness for quick melting)	Salted caramel sauce	Jam, fruit preserves, or marmalade
Anna's Ginger Thins		Nutella	Rainbow sprinkles
Cookies	Andes Crème de Menthe Thins	Bittersweet chocolate sauce	Maple syrup
Pretzels		Dulce de leche	Salted honey
Pizzelle cookies	Reese's Peanut Butter Cups	Peanut butter or another nut butter	Bacon
Matzo	Brownies (cut to fit base with cookie cutter)	Biscoff Cookie Butter	
Flour tortillas		Lemon or lime curd	
Baguette	Best-quality white chocolate	Brie (or another ripe cheese)	

MAKE YOUR FAVORITES

Thank Yous

Thanks to my intrepid agent, Janis Donnaud, for always having my back and connecting me with the best projects.

Heartfelt gratitude to my friend Amanda Hesser and her copilot Merrill Stubbs for thinking of me for this book and charging me with the lucky task of several months of backyard cooking, and to the team at Food52 for embracing the idea. It's been a pleasure to volley ideas and one-liners, and to work within your abundantly talented hive mind.

I feel so fortunate to have worked with book editor Ali Slagle, who made this journey impossibly fun, diffused stress at every turn, and elevated this project with her whip-smart suggestions, fearless grilling, and gorgeous food styling. And that box of homemade cookies, at the eleventh hour, to fuel me to the finish line? Raising the bar on every level, Ali!

Thanks to the dream team at Ten Speed Press for enthusiastically embracing a new perspective on grilling and improving it with their sharp filter. I hope there's an ice luge in your future, Julie Bennett.

Thanks to the stellar photo shoot team who made the book in your hands such a stunner, including photographer James Ransom, creative director Kristen Miglore, art director Alexis Anthony, stylist Sarah Jampel, shoot producer Amanda Widis, and cooks Josh Cohen, Allison Buford, Caroline Lange, and Paige Reinis.

Thanks to the team at PK Grills, especially Scott Moody. My PK360 truly is the "best and last grill I'll ever own," and I know ours is the beginning of a beautiful, smoke-infused friendship. Thanks to Dennis Powell at Butter Pat Industries for making our meals more beautiful with the world's sexiest cast-iron skillet.

Thanks to Aaron Franklin, my mentor for cooking over fire, for indulging my many texts, questions, and food photos, and for generously sharing your expertise. Thanks to Stacy and Vivian Franklin for enthusiastic hot dog condiment feedback, and for always making me laugh.

Thanks to chef friends who shared their expertise via recipes and/or tips, including Susan Spicer, Todd Duplechan and Jessica Maher, Tim Byres, Johnny Hernandez, and Drew and Mary Catherine Curren. Thanks to Gabrielle Hamilton for sharing wisecracks, grill smarts, and cocktail musings while I was hanging out back cooking dinner.

Thanks to friends who came over for meals on the back porch to offer feedback and moral support, and to those who test-drove my recipes, including Amy Brotman, Greg Lane, Pat Sharpe, Charles Lohrmann, Nancy Mims and Rodney Gibbs, Jen Moreno, Brandi Nelson, Ashley Hawkins, Elizabeth and Thomas Winslow, Amanda Eyre Ward and Tip Meckel, Claiborne Smith, Tomas Rivera, Veronica Koltuniak, Annette Patterson, Abigail King, Clayton Maxwell, Joshua and Jamie LaRue, and Rachel Zindler and Paul Newman. Thanks to my friends at Foodways Texas (hi Marvin Bendele and Robb Walsh) for inviting me to Barbecue Boot Camp.

Thanks to my parents, Mike and Julie Disbrowe, for always cheering me on, and for enduring the endless roller coaster of recipe testing (and hours spent in coffee shops chasing deadlines) that my crazy profession requires. Thanks to my brothers, Tim and Tyler Disbrowe, for finding it perfectly normal to spend endless hours discussing smoked pork shoulder and spareribs.

Thanks to Fran Norman, Jana Norman, and Paul Turley for love and support from Pensacola and Adelaide. There's a heap of grilled Gulf shrimp and grouper on our horizon.

Deepest gratitude to my family: My wonderful children, Flannery and Wyatt, for being so cool about all the time that Mom spent racing through grocery stores, schlepping charcoal and firing up dinner, and for rolling with the schedule when dinners went a bit late. Thanks for moving music lessons and playtime outdoors to so we could spend time together throughout the process. Finally, thanks to my husband, David Norman, for being my constant sounding board, making those last-minute runs for charcoal and propane, and for letting me take over the backyard shift. I still think you make the best chicken thighs. The moment when the three of you pull up a seat to our dinner table will always be the best part of any day.

Index

All rights reserved.
Published in the United States by Ten Speed Press,
an imprint of the Crown Publishing Group,
a division of Penguin Random House LLC, New York.
www.crownpublishing.com
www.tenspeed.com

Ten Speed Press and the Ten Speed Press colophon are
registered trademarks of Penguin Random House LLC.

Some of the material in this work first appeared on the Food52 website.

Library of Congress Cataloging-in-Publication Data
Names: Disbrowe, Paula, author. | Ransom, James (Photographer)
Title: Food52 any night grilling : 60 ways to fire up dinner (and more) /
  Paula Disbrowe ; photography by James Ransom.
  Other titles: Food fifty-two any night grilling
Description: First edition. | California : Ten Speed Press, [2017] |
  Includes index.
Identifiers: LCCN 2017028346
Subjects: LCSH: Barbecuing. | Cooking (Smoked foods) | LCGFT: Cookbooks.
Classification: LCC TX840.B3 D57 2017 | DDC 641.7/6—dc23
LC record available at https://lccn.loc.gov/2017028346

Hardcover ISBN: 978-1-5247-5896-7
eBook ISBN: 978-1-5247-5897-4

Printed in China

Design by Margaux Keres

10 9 8 7 6 5 4 3 2 1

First Edition